GRILL
SMOKE
BBQ

CONTENTS

TAMING THE FLAME

Setting out on this project was very exciting for us at Ember Yard, and we were determined to make it different (hopefully) from other barbecue books out there, and to show you how versatile barbecuing can be. Venturing beyond the ubiquitous pulled pork, brisket and wings – yes, these are there too – we've favoured lighter dishes, with more fish, vegetables and even desserts, all making the most of the barbecue's magic.

My own passion for grilling over charcoal and wood is deep-seated, but it began in a typically British fashion. When I was growing up, the annual dusting down of the family barbecue and its utensils at the beginning of summer may have been predictable, but it was still full of expectation. Back then it was more about the ceremony of lighting the fire and the anticipation, rather than the actual results: dubious sausages and 70%-meat-content(!) burgers; perhaps some very well-done, leathery steak; and a nod to the vegetarians, with some corn-on-the-cob.

Fast forward to the present. The ceremony is still as exciting as ever – something to do with our primal instinct to light a fire for cooking, the smell of smoke and the lick of flame almost hypnotizing. But now it's all about the flavour: the smoky, rich taste of food cooked over an open fire is one of life's true pleasures, and there's really nothing like it.

Whether you're cooking herb-stuffed sea bream, a rare-breed Dexter rib steak, a whole chicken, or an anchovy-spiked leg of lamb, the charcoal and wood work their magic.

Having travelled through many parts of Spain and Italy – including the Basque Country, Rioja, Tuscany and Piedmont – I've witnessed first-hand the true art of grilling. In these regions, cooking over an open flame is second nature, and many houses and restaurants have a grilling contraption out the back, or indeed in the actual kitchen.

One of the best pieces of beef I've ever eaten was a Chianina T-bone grilled over the simplest of fires in Florence's Trattoria Sostanza, the meat expertly blackened and gently perfumed with smoke from hazel-wood charcoal. The two guys running the grill were captivating in their deftness and skill (not to mention their ability to hang a fag from their lips throughout), and completely in tune with the natural rhythm of the fire and smoke.

Traditional Basque grills especially fascinate me, with their distinctive operating wheel that precisely raises or lowers the grilling racks to allow food to be cooked quickly, slowly, or anything in between. Chef Victor Arguinzoniz of Asador Etxebarri, in the rolling hills of the Basque countryside, has turned grilling into a true artform. He is in control of the entire process, from chopping down the various trees for the wood, drying the logs and then burning them in a furnace to make the charcoal. Victor even designed his own custom Basque grill to meet his exacting requirements. Perhaps unsurprisingly, then, the food from Etxebarri is some of the best I've had. It's incredibly simple, just one or two elements on the plate, and that's it – but these elements all have a controlled, balanced and relevant smokiness to them that could only come from Victor's intuitive cooking and years of practice.

Etxebarri is a unique experience, and one that can't really be replicated, not least because of its location – a backdrop of a grassy mountainside dotted with Basque sheep makes it an ethereal experience! However, much can be learnt from this approach, even by a novice: the importance of sourcing the best ingredients you can find, along with natural (chemical-free) charcoal and a fundamental understanding of how fire and smoke work...

Nowadays, excellent produce is available from artisan butchers, fishmongers, grocers and even some supermarkets, so there's no need to go down the dodgy sausage route any more – unless you really feel compelled to. And there's plenty of wonderful, slow-burning charcoal out there – we like to use single-species varieties of charcoal, such as oak, silver birch, hazel and apple. Their subtle flavours permeate the food without any overpowering acridity, and you can experiment by matching specific woods with different foods. Great fun.

So, what to cook on? Times have changed, and the choice of barbecues is staggering! The masses have embraced the Weber, kettle-style barbecue and all the accessories that go with it, right down to the gloves and tongs. And very good they are too: the chimney starter is a genius idea, speeding up the whole lighting process and enabling you to top up the coals as you go. Then there's the Big Green Egg, which is very special but also very expensive, thanks to its NASA-designed insulation that lets you crank up the heat to ridiculously high temperatures. At Ember Yard – our grill restaurant in Berwick Street, Soho – we use a pimped-up Robata-style grill, as favoured by the Japanese. Our new one is a beast, with a wheel and hoist to raise it up and lower it down for different cooking styles, and it really is the business. But actually all you need is a sturdy, robust barbecue with a large surface area, and a lid so you can smoke food. Personally, I'm not a huge fan of the gas barbecue, but if you have one, by all means use it for these recipes; you'll just end up with different flavours.

We want to encourage you to think of barbecuing
and grilling as a year-round method of cooking – just
an extension of the way you cook in your kitchen,
using what's best and in season. Don't be afraid to
light the coals on a cold winter's afternoon.

Yes, it may be chilly, but wrap up warm and get cooking – you can
always eat inside. Besides, the British summer is usually way too
short to miss out on the fantastic smoky flavours and ceremony of
cooking over charcoal and wood at other times of the year.

Of course, stereotypically, barbecuing is seen as a male-
dominated pastime, but we think otherwise. We hope the
contents of this book will make the whole experience easy and
fun for everyone to try. It's time to embrace the barbecue and
grill! Move on from the ubiquitous summer barbecues and take it
up a gear, whatever the weather.

A practical note on using this book

Nearly all these recipes involve using the barbecue one way
or another. Some dishes, such as the larger sharing plates, are
cooked entirely on the barbecue, while for others, just one or
two elements might be barbecued.

Of course, it's not really practical to wheel out the barbecue,
light and set it just to grill some strawberries for dessert
(although I've been guilty of that before!), so I encourage you
to use the barbecue for a full meal, or a few dishes, perhaps
cooking something else in advance, to make the most of the
effort involved.

Some of the recipes are quick to prepare and cook, while others
require more time for smoking, marinating or brining, followed by
a longer cooking time. It's best to read a recipe through first and
find out what suits the timeframe you have in mind. Personally,
I love getting stuck into a couple of recipes over the weekend that
require time and prep and make a fun project of it.

While you can make many of these dishes using a stovetop
chargrill pan in the kitchen, their soul comes from cooking them
over the open flame – with charcoal, wood and smoke.

CHOOSING AND USING YOUR BARBECUE

Once upon a time, more than likely when the first summer sun had just popped out, I'd wheel out the rusting barbecue, brush away the cobwebs and burnt-sausage debris and load up the barbecue with briquettes I'd bought from the local garage. It didn't really occur to me that this piece of borderline scrap could enhance the flavour of food as it cooked and be used to create some sublime dishes.

There's nothing remotely complicated here, but it's probably the most important section in this book, and I'd recommend you read it before you get started. This will really show you how to make the most of your barbecue and what you cook on it.

Not wanting to complicate things, I decided to use two simple barbecues to cook everything in this book: one a round kettle-style barbecue with a 56cm (22in) cooking area; the other a rectangular drum-style barbecue with an 80 x 54cm (32 x 21in) cooking area. Each has a lid, top and bottom vents, a built-in thermometer and one level of grill; to control the heat, food is moved from one side to the other, rather than up and down. If your barbecue has an upper grill shelf, that can also be useful for resting meat or fish after cooking and for keeping food warm.

One point worth mentioning is size: a larger barbecue can obviously hold bigger things; if you want to cook a whole fish and some vegetables, then a smaller one won't do. The dimensions of the barbecues mentioned above are big enough to cope with anything called for in these recipes – and if you've got two fired up at the same time, then the world's your oyster. For example, when I'm cooking a dinner party for a few friends, I'll have both barbecues going, so I can cook the different elements at the same time – rather like having two ovens and the stovetop working simultaneously.

Barbecues and accessories

The barbecue you choose will depend on your preference, style and budget, but as long as it is sturdily built, and has a lid and vents, you are ready to roll. If your chosen barbecue doesn't have a built-in thermometer, you can easily buy one separately – and it's well worth it, especially for cooking larger items like joints of meat.

I've mentioned Weber and the Big Green Egg (see page 9). I also recommend the Drumbecue. Look up their websites (see page 250) for their ranges and stockists.

If you're a barbecuing novice, start with some simple, functional kit. As you progress and get more into the art of cooking over charcoal and wood, you can add to your equipment and accessories as you see fit – there really is a whole world of equipment out there.

Other kit I recommend without going mad (no combat-style barbecue attire required here!) are:

- **temperature probe**, for checking when meat is done – especially chicken, which needs to be cooked through properly
- two good, solid pairs of **tongs**, at least one pair with long handles
- **poker**, to stoke the fire
- **fish-grilling basket**, for cooking larger, flat fish – highly recommended, as it's tricky to cook them without sticking otherwise
- sturdy **fish slice** or **spatula**
- **barbecue brush**, for basting and brushing marinades and oil onto food as it cooks
- **barbecue gloves** – go for heatproof gloves, as opposed to the more cumbersome mitts
- large and sturdy **two-pronged fork**
- **wire brush**, for keeping the grill nice and clean

I also like to have some short wooden planks to hand, such as you might cut from old floorboards. When soaked for a few hours, these are really good for sitting cakes and tarts on when you're baking over the coals; the damp wood acts as a perfect heat diffuser, so that the outside of whatever you're cooking doesn't get scorched. This pleasingly low-tech solution was discovered after much frustration and several burnt tarts while developing and testing the recipes for this book...

Lighting your barbecue

A charcoal chimney starter is by far the best, easiest and most economical way to light a barbecue, I think. Simply put a couple of firelighters in the centre of your barbecue and place the chimney on top. The 'chimney effect' will light the coals evenly all the way through the chimney, so they are ready to be tipped straight into your barbecue. The coals are ready for cooking when they are uniformly ashen grey. One load should be sufficient for a 56–60cm (22–23in) barbecue and will happily cook whatever you throw at it for around 2 hours. A chimney starter is also great for topping up the barbecue if you want to keep cooking for several hours; just re-light the chimney (separately from the barbecue), then use the fresh batch of coals to top up the barbecue, so you have continuous heat.

The alternative is the good old-fashioned and perfectly acceptable method of spreading a layer of charcoal in the desired area of the barbecue, dotting a few firelighters here and there and lighting them. This is then followed up with more chunks of charcoal on top. When the charcoal has turned ashen grey, you are ready to cook.

Setting the barbecue for direct/indirect cooking

Now is when you start to make a difference in terms of how and what you cook. Whether you are using a rectangular drum-style barbecue or a round kettle-style barbecue, the cooking area can be differentiated into two zones.

If all you want to do is fast grilling, simply fill the base of your barbecue with charcoal, then light as described above. This is known as **direct cooking**, as you are cooking directly over the hot coals.

Leaving a charcoal-free space of, say, a half or a third of the barbecue, allows for **direct/indirect cooking**. This enables you to grill or sear in the direct heat zone and then finish the cooking in the indirect heat zone, which is a slower-cooking, more oven-like environment. With indirect cooking – and some direct cooking – the lid of the barbecue needs to be closed, in order to capture the heat and smoke.

Larger cuts of meat that need long and slow cooking can also be started from scratch on the indirect heat zone where, over time, they will develop caramelization, rather like a roast chicken or leg of pork in a conventional oven. Some foods have a tendency to dry out during this lengthy cooking, however; to avoid this, sit a deep baking tray or roasting tin, or one of those disposable foil trays in the direct heat zone, next to whatever it is you're cooking, and fill it two-thirds-full with water. This will create steam and a moist environment, which will help the cooking process. I've mentioned this in the recipes where I think it's necessary.

Direct Cooking

Indirect Cooking

Controlling the heat

All charcoal barbecues have two vents: one at the top and one at the bottom or side. These should remain open during cooking for maximum heat, as they allow air to flow throughout the barbecue, which fuels the fire. If the barbecue is getting too hot and you want to moderate the heat, close the vents slightly to reduce the flow of air. Only fully close the vents when you want to smother the flames and kill the barbecue, or when you are cold-smoking. Controlling the heat in this way is something you'll master and get comfortable with over time and as your confidence increases.

Setting the barbecue for direct/indirect cooking gives you a range of cooking temperatures and zones, and with experience you'll soon understand how the various zones work – the hottest, of course, being in the middle of the direct heat zone, and the coolest at the perimeter of the indirect heat zone, with everything else in between. This range of temperatures is really useful when cooking more than one dish or multiple elements of a single dish.

Coolest Zone

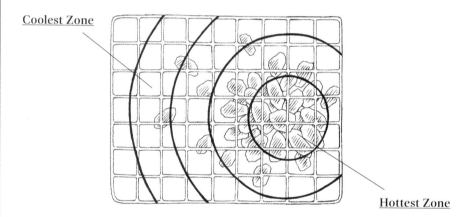

Hottest Zone

Using wood on the barbecue

It's by no means essential to throw logs or wood chips on your barbecue. Charcoal alone will cook things just fine. The use of wood is all about adding flavour and smoke (see page 20–21). Throughout the book, I've included suggestions for using wood chips or wood dust in the cold-smoker; or wood chips, lumps and even small logs on the barbecue, to hot-smoke food as it cooks.

Ember cooking

This is a great way of cooking fruit and vegetables with a high water content. Burying the wrapped food in the embers helps to intensify its flavours by reducing the moisture content, and the moisture in turn helps to prevent burning. Simply wrap your fruit or vegetables in foil and nestle the parcels in the embers after the fire has died down. Ensure the parcel is completely smothered with the hot coals to get the full effect and ensure it will cook evenly.

WOOD AND CHARCOAL

Wood and charcoal are the means through which the dishes are cooked, smoked and flavoured. So it's only appropriate to give some thought to sourcing the right wood and charcoal for what you are cooking – just as you would when choosing a piece of beef from the butchers, a glistening fresh bream from the fishmonger's slab or a beautifully ripe fresh fig.

Wood

It all starts with the wood (even the charcoal). When buying lump wood, make sure it's hardwood, as softwood tends to burn with an unpleasant, acrid note. The wood should be already seasoned or dried, meaning the moisture has evaporated and will be easy to burn. Wood chips and wood dust are a little more specialized, but are easy enough to find online.

You'll probably buy your wood from the same place as your charcoal, so you should be able to find out what variety it is and where it's from. There's lots of fun to be had by experimenting with different kinds of wood, and my guide on the page opposite should help you on your way.

Charcoal

So what is charcoal? Essentially, it's wood that has been turned into coal by a fairly complex distillation process. A bag of lump-wood charcoal will generally be made from a mix of oak, beech and ash that has been heated to a high temperature in a sealed environment. Starved of oxygen, the wood releases water and gases, resulting in a light, yet concentrated fuel that is better all-round than the compressed, chemically enhanced briquettes. Because no artificial starters are used in its production, the flavour of foods is enhanced, rather than masked by a chemical aftertaste; and the charcoal burns longer and brighter, making it more economical. With transparent and ethical sourcing, it is also kinder to the environment.

Single-species wood and charcoal

If you want to delve deeper, there are many varieties of single-species wood and charcoal out there to experiment with – these can impart impressive flavours when paired with different foods.

Mark Parr at London Log Company has been slowly pioneering this movement in the UK over recent years, and is now the go-to charcoal and wood guru for progressive chefs and enthusiastic novices alike. All Mark's wood and charcoal is sourced and produced in the UK, and he has a fascinating and constantly evolving range of single-species charcoal that really does seem to give barbecued food a special clarity of flavour.

Below are some examples of what I've found works well, whether you're cold- or hot-smoking with hardwood or cooking directly over charcoal. This should be used as a rough guide and to inspire new combinations. Remember, smoking is not a science, it's an artform!

OAK I've found oak to be a great all-rounder for cooking meat, fish and vegetables. It imparts a pronounced earthy/woody flavor, while still letting the main ingredients shine through.

APPLE Apple wood is quite delicate, which makes it great for cooking white fish; the wood chips are great for cold-smoking too. Perhaps unsurprisingly, apple wood has a natural affinity with fatty pork, and we love to pair it with hot-smoked pork belly.

BAY This produces a subtle floral flavour that's good with fish and vegetables.

BEECH Another good all-rounder with a fragrant, almost musky smoke.

BIRCH A mild wood with a delicate aroma that's perfect for cold-smoking fish.

CHERRY Try this light, sweet smoke with duck, chicken and meaty fish.

CHESTNUT A medium-strength, nutty-flavoured wood that's nice to use during the colder months.

HICKORY A classic barbecue wood that imparts a strong flavour. I'd only use this with more robust food, such as red meats and stronger-tasting fish.

THE NOT-SO-MYSTIFYING ART OF SMOKING

This book wouldn't be complete without some words on one of our very best friends at Ember Yard: smoke. The main reason we love cooking over a charcoal- or wood-fired barbecue is the chance to capture some of that ethereal smokiness in whatever we are cooking.

Smoke and fire are intrinsically linked, of course, and a good understanding of both will elevate your cooking skills on the barbecue to a new level. Yes, you can simply grill over some charcoal, and that's fine, but the real essence of barbecuing lies in harnessing the natural flavours from burning wood and charcoal in this process. Throw a chunk of wood or some wood chips onto your barbecue, close the lid, and you will get some intense smoky flavours happening on top of the flavour from the charcoal. Essentially, that's all there is to it – but with a little know-how and understanding, you can turn your barbecue into something much more than the sum of its parts. Be warned – it's highly addictive once you get going.

Introducing foodstuffs to smoke is a centuries-old process: perhaps a side-effect of cooking over an open fire; the result of hanging meat to dry near campfires; or even a mistake. If a mistake, it was a fortunate one, for not only does the smoke impart a sublime flavour but it also acts as a natural preservative, which would have been incredibly important in the days before refrigeration. Later, the use of salt and brines prolonged shelf-life even further, as well as adding their own flavour. It's interesting that one of the earliest-known methods of cooking and preserving is now the height of fashion in gastronomic circles and you'll find smoke in just about everything from cocktails and ice creams to fruit and chocolate!

Smoke comes from the burning of hardwoods and, to a lesser degree, charcoal (wood that's already had most of its natural gases burnt off, to make a highly concentrated fuel). When wood is burnt, water, natural gases and carbon are released, and the lignin in the wood breaks down to produce the sweet smoke associated with barbecues. When choosing your wood and charcoal (see pages 20–21), it's worth remembering that it's this smoke that will end up flavouring your food.

Smoking will never be an exact science, and there'll always be an element of trial and error – at least until you get more confident – but there's no reason you can't successfully smoke food at home. At the restaurant, we have purpose-built hot- and cold-smokers that consistently produce well-rounded smoked flavours, so we can be confident of what we serve our customers. Of course, at some point you might want to consider investing in (or even building) a smaller-scale specialist smoker – such as the ProQ cold-smoke generator: you simply fill the gadget with wood dust, light it and pop it in your barbecue, then it slowly releases cool smoke over a period of a few hours. Until then, if you have a barbecue with a lid, an empty tin and a temperature probe, you're all set.

There are two main methods of smoking food: hot-smoking and cold-smoking.

Hot-smoking

Hot-smoking flavours the surface of the food while cooking it at the same time – but at temperatures of 52–80°C (125–175°F), the process will be long and slow. This suits some of the larger cuts of meat that contain enough fat to self-baste as they cook, such as lamb shoulder, pork belly or oxtail. Arguably, this kind of hot-smoking is the essence of barbecuing, and embodies all that is rich, delicious and unctuous about slow-cooked meats.

I recommend soaking wood chips or hardwood lumps in cold water before adding them to the hot coals: an hour will suffice for wood chips, and a few hours for lumps. What this does is stop the wood from incinerating and burning fiercely on impact; instead, it will start to smoke gently.

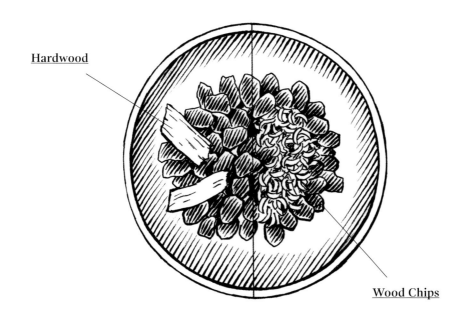

Hardwood

Wood Chips

Generally, I add wood chips when I'm cooking something relatively quickly, to add a short, sharp burst of smoke; and lumps of hardwood (about 8cm (3in) quarters) if I'm cooking something for longer, with the bigger pieces of wood slowly but surely doing their thing over time.

I've indicated in the recipes when to add wood chips or hardwood lumps, but there are no hard-and-fast rules. Feel free to experiment by adding wood when and where you see fit. Just remember to wait until the flames have died down and the charcoal has achieved the all-important ashen-grey stage for optimum cooking. If you are using wood chips, sprinkle them directly onto the coals. If you are using lumps of hardwood, carefully nestle them into the coals, using long-handled tongs or a poker to carefully push a little of the perimeter ash around the wood to 'pen it in' – this helps the wood to smoke nicely and for longer.

Cold-smoking

In this process, smoke penetrates the food without actually cooking it as the temperature doesn't exceed 30°C (86°F). We use this technique for introducing a subtle, smoky flavour to fish, vegetables and even liquids over a period of 1–2 hours. We also like to cold-smoke meat and meatier fish prior to cooking it on the grill. This gives two layers of smokiness on eating: an intrinsic background smokiness from the cold-smoking, then a more pronounced hit from the barbecuing process.

For easy cold-smoking on your barbecue, all you need is a small perforated firebox (many barbecues come with these) or a clean empty can (from beans, tuna and so on), with the lid prised open. Use a screwdriver to – carefully! – poke a few holes in the lid, then half-fill the can or firebox with your choice of wood chips (see page 21). Using long-handled tongs, carefully add a piece of very hot charcoal and then cover it with more wood chips. Close the lid of the can or firebox and sit it in one corner of your barbecue. Position a grill rack above it and place whatever you're smoking on the rack. Close the barbecue lid, making sure the top vent is closed, and leave for the time specified in the recipe – although it's always good to check the temperature inside the barbecue as a back-up.

After cold-smoking, always give food a resting time of at least 6 hours (or overnight) before eating it or cooking it further. This allows the smoky flavours to develop and balance out.

This book has a good few recipes that involve cold-smoking but once you've mastered the process, experiment and see what works for you. Often, you'll find that ingredients that have been marinated, salted or brined (see Basics on page 242–243) tend to hold the smoke flavour better.

BARBECUES AND BOOZE

The sad stereotype of 'Barbecue Man' is etched into our psyches: with a T-shirt and striped apron stretched across his pot belly, his sunburnt arms hold tongs in one hand and a cold beer in the other. But it needn't be like this. We like to enjoy cocktails and wines while grilling and barbecuing. And it's great fun to use the barbecue and its cooking fuel (wood, smoke, charcoal) to create garnishes and infusions for cocktails, alcoholic or not.

Why not quickly chargrill citrus fruit peel to make a smoky, zesty garnish for a cocktail, G&T or otherwise? Or get adventurous and infuse your neglected (or perhaps not!) bottle of bourbon with some barbecue-smoked bacon rind, leave it to steep for a few days and then knock up a smoky, savoury twist on an Old Fashioned. If you're cold-smoking, try putting a tray of water into the barbecue to smoke for an hour, before freezing it to create smoked ice – this works wonders in a Bloody Mary or Manhattan.

When cooking with hardwood, once it burns down to solid charcoal embers, carefully fish one out with long-handled tongs, set it aside to cool and use it to infuse spirits or liqueurs. Or drop a handful of twiggy herbs (thyme, rosemary, oregano or marjoram) onto your hot grill for a few seconds and use them to infuse liquids or olive oil. Using a mortar and pestle, grind some good, single-species charcoal to a powder, ready for sprinkling over cocktails.

As for pairing wines, the basic rule of thumb is that fuller-bodied reds are more conducive to winter climes, larger cuts of red meat and game; in warmer months, lighter reds work better. So when barbecuing in the depths of winter, uncork a full-bodied red Rioja to accompany a large succulent grilled T-bone. In summer, lightly chill a medium-bodied red like Pinot Noir to accompany your red meat spread. When it comes to white wines, fuller-bodied and oak-aged varieties work well with full-flavoured, charred or smoked white meat and fish. Equally, light and zesty whites go down a treat with simply grilled fish, such as sardines with lemon and olive oil. If you're on a splurge, and have got a lobster on the grill, open a crisp, smoky white with mineral notes – we especially like wines of this type from the Campania region of southern Italy.

The basic message here is that when it comes to booze and barbecues, the guidelines are just a guide. The real fun comes from experimenting – and demolishing that stereotype once and for all.

It's time to explore some of the many alternative ways to enjoy booze with a barbecue. It doesn't have to be a beer-only affair, and there's certainly no need for barbecues to be male-dominated drinking sanctuaries.

BREAKFAST, BRUNCH & BREAD

I love weekend breakfasts at home. For me, this is a time for relaxation, family and the chance to cook something delicious.

Make your weekend breakfast an occasion and start the day as you mean to go on.

But would you really get the barbecue out for breakfast, I hear you ask. Well, why not? Once you've got your barbecue lit, popped the coffee on, maybe mixed a Bloody Mary, read the papers and got everything ready, the barbecue will be at optimum temperature and ready to roll. Just imagine cooking fennel-infused sausages, glistening, fatty pancetta and even frying golden-yolked eggs over the glowing heat of the charcoal, everything benefiting from the faint lick and wisp of smoke from the charcoal and wood... Cooking breakfast or brunch over a barbecue will make the weekend (or a weekday off) even more special. And it doesn't have to be summer. If it's nippy outside, just set the table inside and bring in the food (or get everyone to man-up and put on their thermals!), so you can still experience the amazing barbecue flavours.

We don't offer breakfast at Ember Yard, but we do serve brunch, and some of the dishes in this section have appeared on our brunch menu at some stage or in slightly different guises – our takes on the classic English breakfast have become legendary with hungover weekend Soho-ites and hungry local shoppers. Try charcoal-grilled pancetta with fried eggs and chorizo ketchup for starters, then add a potato, honey and thyme flatbread for good measure!

There's also a selection of pizzette, or mini-pizzas, which we encourage you to try. Once you've got the knack, diversify and experiment as much as you like. Flatbreads work brilliantly cooked over charcoal, as their large surface area means they take on plenty of smoky goodness. Serve them straight from the grill, nice and hot, doused in a punchy, garlicky pesto or our signature smoked butter, which is easily mastered using the cold-smoking technique on page 25. The Turkish pide, blackberries and creamed sheep's cheese recipe is something I brought back with me from indulgent food-led holidays in Alaçatı, on Turkey's Aegean Coast, where the breakfasts are second to none. Blackberries slowly simmered and turned to jam over charcoal take on a smoky note, while the hot, grilled Turkish bread and the cool, creamy cheese bring everything together beautifully.

There are also some deliciously healthy options, with mackerel and sardines making an appearance. Rich in omega 3s, both of these oily fish barbecue beautifully, their skins blistering and their natural oils self-basting the flesh. As they cook, they give off a heady aroma evocative of summers spent by the sea in Portugal and Spain, or on the banks of the Bosphorus in Istanbul, where charcoal-grilled mackerel sandwiches are served to what seems like the entire population on their way to work. When it comes to flavour and nutrients, sardines and mackerel are truly the champions of fish – and even better, they are currently very sustainable.

Finally, I couldn't skip giving a nod to the US (we are barbecuing, after all), with some light and fluffy buttermilk-based pancakes – here given a whole new dimension with the addition of some char and smoke...

So, it's the weekend and you've some time on your hands: get the charcoal lit, toss on a few chunks of wood and let the barbecue take care of breakfast. It's a no-brainer.

Baked eggs with chorizo, tomato, peppers and spinach

This is a great one-pot job for a lazy breakfast or brunch. Cooking chorizo (or parrilla chorizo, as it's known in Spain) is best for this recipe. Only semi-cured, it needs to be cooked, releasing all its smoky-porky goodness and melting into the tomato sauce as it goes. Serve this with some toasted sourdough for dipping.

Light and set the barbecue for direct/indirect cooking.

Place a medium-sized ovenproof frying pan or flameproof casserole on the grill in the direct heat zone. Add a lug of olive oil and cook the onion and garlic, without colouring, for 3–4 minutes. If the pan gets too hot, move it off the direct heat zone to control the temperature. Next add the pepper and chorizo and cook for 3–4 minutes until the chorizo has softened and released its paprika-rich juices.

Add the tomatoes and move the pan to the indirect heat zone. Close the lid and cook slowly (the temperature inside the barbecue should be about 200°C/400°F) for about 30–35 minutes, stirring occasionally, until reduced and thickened.

Check the seasoning and adjust as needed, then stir in the spinach. Use the back of a spoon to make 4 hollows and crack in the eggs. Close the lid of the barbecue and cook for 4–5 minutes or until the egg whites are just set but the yolks are still runny. Season the eggs with salt and pepper. Serve immediately.

Serves 4

1 large onion, finely chopped
2 large garlic cloves, finely chopped
1 large red (bell) pepper, deseeded and roughly chopped
150g (5½oz) spicy cooking chorizo, roughly chopped
700g (1lb 8oz) very ripe tomatoes, roughly chopped
1 large handful young spinach leaves
4 free-range eggs
olive oil, for cooking
sea salt and black pepper

Pizzette bases

Basically mini-pizzas, pizzette are a great size for brunch or as part of a feast. As long as you have a hot clean grill, the pizzette bases can be cooked directly on this before the toppings (see page 39–40) are added and the cooking finished at a lower temperature to the side. Who would have thought of barbecued pizza? Yet it works fantastically and you get the proper smoky flavours of a wood-fired oven. This recipe makes enough dough for 10 pizzette. Any leftover dough can be kept in the fridge, wrapped in cling film, for a few days.

Whisk the yeast into the lukewarm water to dissolve. In another bowl, combine the flours, salt, sugar and olive oil, then gradually stir in the yeast mixture until the dough starts to come together. On a floured surface, knead with your hands until you have a fairly smooth, elastic dough, then return the dough to the bowl, cover with a damp clean cloth and leave in a warm place for 30 minutes, or until doubled in size.

Evenly divide the dough into 10 balls, then roll out on a lightly floured surface to form small pizzette.

Set the barbecue for direct/indirect cooking and place the lump of wood in the indirect heat zone. Ensure the grill is nice and clean – and very hot – before starting to cook. Lightly oil the pizzette bases on both sides, then carefully place on the grill in the direct heat zone and cook for 2–3 minutes; they should start to puff up and bubble. Turn over and cook for a further 2 minutes before moving to the indirect heat zone. Add your choice of the toppings, then finish cooking as instructed.

Makes 10

You'll also need a lump of oak or beech wood

1 x 7g sachet (2¼ tsp) dried yeast
350ml (1½ cups) lukewarm water
500g (3⅔ cups) white bread flour, sifted
100g (½ cup) semolina flour, sifted
½ tsp fine salt
1½ tsp caster (superfine) sugar
2 Tbsp olive oil

Pizzette with tomato, aubergine, chilli and goat's cheese

Soft, tangy goat's cheese and aubergine is a match made in heaven, and this Sicilian-inspired pizzette has a spicy tomato sauce to give it a real kick! It's best to make the tomato sauce in advance on the stovetop, so it has time to cool and thicken.

Serves 4

4 pizzette bases (see opposite),
  brushed with olive oil
½ small aubergine (eggplant), very
  finely sliced into discs
100g (3½ oz) semi-soft goat's cheese
½ red chilli, finely chopped
6 basil leaves
extra virgin olive oil, for drizzling
sea salt and black pepper

For the tomato sauce
½ onion, finely chopped
1 garlic clove, finely chopped
½ teaspoon dried chilli flakes
400g (14oz) ripe tomatoes, roughly
  chopped
olive oil, for cooking

For the tomato sauce, place a saucepan over medium heat and sweat the onion, garlic and chilli flakes in a little olive oil for 3 minutes or until soft. Add the tomatoes and cook slowly for about 35 minutes to reduce and thicken. Season to taste.

Spread the tomato sauce over the pizzette bases, leaving a small border all around the edges. Lay the aubergine slices on top, crumble on the goat's cheese and sprinkle over the fresh chilli. Season well, then cook for 5 minutes in the indirect heat zone with the lid closed until the aubergine is cooked and the cheese has started to melt.

Drizzle with extra virgin olive oil and tear over the basil leaves before serving.

Pizzette with sprouting broccoli, smoked anchovies, egg and oregano

More classic Italian flavours here. You should be able to buy fantastically sweet, oak-smoked anchovies from good delis and supermarkets, but, failing that, regular salted ones will suffice.

Serves 4

150g (5½oz) sprouting broccoli,
  very finely sliced
4 pizzette bases (see opposite),
  brushed with olive oil
16 smoked or salted anchovies
4 free-range eggs
2 tsp oregano leaves
extra virgin olive oil, for drizzling
sea salt and black pepper

Lay the broccoli on the pizzette bases, then divide the anchovies evenly between them. Crack an egg into the middle of each pizzette. Season well and cook in the indirect heat zone with the lid closed for 5–6 minutes until the broccoli is just tender and the egg whites are set but the yolks are still nice and runny.

Serve drizzled with extra virgin olive oil and scattered with oregano leaves.

Pizzette with nduja, pecorino and fennel

Nduja has become a very trendy ingredient of late; however, this fiery Calabrian sausage paste has been around for centuries. Delicious on pizza, it will certainly wake you up with its chilli kick! A young pecorino that's softer and creamier than the aged sort will work better here, as it will melt more evenly. Alternatively, a good, tasty, soft white cheese from the UK or US would also work well.

Spread the nduja on the pizzette bases, leaving a small border around the edges, then sprinkle over the pecorino and top with the fennel. Season and cook in the indirect heat zone with the lid closed for 8 minutes until the cheese has melted and the fennel is lightly cooked.

Drizzle with extra virgin olive oil and sprinkle over any fronds from the fennel bulb before serving.

Serves 4

180g (6½oz) nduja

4 pizzette bases (see page 38), brushed with olive oil

80g (3oz) young pecorino, finely grated

¼ fennel bulb, very finely sliced, any fronds reserved

extra virgin olive oil, for drizzling

sea salt and black pepper

Charcoal-grilled pancetta and sausage with fried morcilla sandwiches, eggs and chorizo ketchup

Sometimes, a fried breakfast is the only thing that will hit the spot, and there's nothing better than a really good one. However, I'm often disappointed by lacklustre bacon and sausage, or by things I don't really want being on the plate. Everything on the plate should be of the best quality, and certainly not a filler. This has all the usual favourites, but with indulgent twists, including a fried bread and morcilla sandwich that's incredibly naughty. Enjoy responsibly and in moderation!

Light the barbecue and set for direct/indirect cooking.

Place the sausages and morcilla directly on the grill in the direct heat zone and cook for 2 minutes on each side to brown. Transfer to the indirect heat zone, close the lid and cook for 6–7 minutes or until the sausages and morcilla are cooked through. Move the sausages to the side of the indirect heat zone to keep warm. Transfer the morcilla to a bowl and mash into a rough paste, then keep warm.

Place an ovenproof non-stick frying pan in the direct heat zone and add a lug of olive oil and the butter. When the butter is foaming, lay the slices of bread in the pan and brown on both sides. Remove the fried bread from the pan and place in the indirect heat zone to keep warm. Crack the eggs into the frying pan and cook steadily until the whites are set but the yolks are still runny – you may need to move the pan into the indirect heat zone to stop the whites from cooking too quickly. Season the eggs with salt and pepper.

While the eggs are cooking, grill the pancetta in the direct cooking zone for 2–3 minutes on each side until cooked and browned. Spread the morcilla between the two slices of fried bread and cut the sandwich into quarters.

Serve on warm plates, with the chorizo ketchup on the side.

Serves 4 for a good breakfast

8 breakfast sausages from a good butcher – I like Lincolnshire, but pork and leek would be great too
150g (5½oz) morcilla or soft black pudding, skin removed
40g (3 Tbsp) unsalted butter
2 thick slices good-quality white bread
4 free-range eggs
8–12 slices thick-cut smoked pancetta or smoked streaky bacon
olive oil, for cooking
sea salt and black pepper
Chorizo ketchup (see page 245), to serve

Smoky eggs with asparagus and sweet shallots on sourdough

Eggs carry smoke wonderfully well. Here they're par-boiled, then set on the barbecue with some wood chips to boost the smokiness, and matched with seasonal asparagus (for me, a highlight of the culinary calendar) – a classic combination. Slowly grilling the asparagus concentrates the natural sugars and intensifies the flavours.

Light the barbecue and set for direct/indirect cooking.

On the stovetop, soft-boil the eggs and then immediately transfer into ice-cold water to arrest the cooking process.

Place a small saucepan over medium heat on the stovetop and add the butter, olive oil and shallots. When the butter starts to bubble, turn the heat down to low and cook the shallots very gently for about an hour or until very tender and lightly caramelized. Season to taste, then add the vinegar and keep warm.

Carefully peel the eggs and place one in each hole of the muffin pan. Place the muffin pan in the indirect heat zone, then sprinkle a good handful of wood chips directly onto the coals. Close the lid and vent of the barbecue and leave the eggs to smoke for 3 minutes. Open the lid, carefully turn the eggs and add another handful of wood chips, then close the lid again and cook for another 3 minutes. Lift the lid to check the eggs – they should have smoked to a brown-orange hue. Move them to the indirect heat zone to keep warm.

Toss the asparagus in olive oil and season well. Place on the grill in the direct heat zone and cook for 2–3 minutes on each side until just tender and lightly charred. Transfer to the indirect heat zone, then grill the bread slices in the direct heat zone until lightly browned.

Spoon the caramelized shallots onto the grilled bread, then top with the asparagus and a smoked egg. Just before serving, break each egg gently with a fork and season with a little salt and pepper.

Serves 4

You'll also need a muffin pan with at least four 10cm (4in) diameter holes and some apple or maple wood chips

4 large free-range eggs
50g (3½ Tbsp) unsalted butter
2 Tbsp extra virgin olive oil
8 banana shallots, very finely sliced
30ml (2 Tbsp) white balsamic or muscatel vinegar
about 12 spears of asparagus, ends and any woody parts of stalks removed
4 slices sourdough bread
olive oil, for cooking
sea salt and black pepper

Grilled buttermilk and chestnut pancakes with pancetta and honey

This American brunch classic has been given an unusual and delicious twist with the addition of a little chestnut flour, sliced fresh chestnuts and chestnut honey. I like to cook the pancakes first and then quickly grill them over the charcoal before topping with some smoky grilled pancetta. If you're feeling naughty, you could make this super-deluxe with the addition of fresh blueberries and some thick organic yogurt or clotted cream.

First make the pancake batter. Stir together the flours, bicarbonate of soda and salt, then add the melted butter. Lightly whisk in the buttermilk, leaving the batter slightly lumpy. Set aside to rest for 20 minutes before cooking.

Light the barbecue and set for direct/indirect cooking.

Place a medium non-stick frying pan in the direct heat zone and, when it is hot, add a ladleful of the pancake batter – it will be quite thick, so you'll need to spread the batter around the pan with a spoon or spatula. Cook for 2 minutes until set, then turn and cook for 2 minutes on the other side. Transfer the cooked pancake to the indirect heat zone to keep warm while you make the rest.

Once you've made all the pancakes, place them on the grill in the direct heat zone for 1 minute on each side. Grill the pancetta slices on both sides until cooked through and a little crispy.

Serve the pancakes with the pancetta on top, finishing with a good drizzle of honey and the fresh chestnuts, if you're using them.

Serves 4 (makes 4 large pancakes)

12 slices medium-cut smoked pancetta or smoked streaky bacon

2 Tbsp chestnut or blossom honey

2 fresh chestnuts, roasted, peeled and roughly chopped – optional

For the pancake batter

100g (¾ cup) plain (all-purpose) flour, sifted

25g (3 Tbsp) chestnut flour, sifted

1 tsp bicarbonate of soda (baking soda)

1 tsp fine salt

50g (3½ Tbsp) unsalted butter, melted

250ml (1 cup) buttermilk

Grilled mackerel with fennel, yogurt and sumac salad

A perfect summer brunch inspired by the flavours of the Levant. Shaved fennel makes for an interesting salad, and the sumac brings a wonderful zesty citrus hit to it all. Check that your mackerel is spanking fresh before you buy – it should be plump, firm and bright, its skin almost effervescent. The fresher the fish, the better it will grill.

Light the barbecue and set for direct cooking.

Like sardines, the skin on mackerel is quite delicate, so make sure your grill is clean and hot to help avoid sticking. Rub the mackerel with olive oil and season with salt and pepper, then place on the grill in the direct heat zone. Cook for 4 minutes on each side, or until the skin is crispy and charred and the flesh is starting to become opaque. Mackerel benefits from being left a little pink in the middle. Rest the fish for 2 minutes before serving.

For the salad, toast the fennel seeds in a dry frying pan over a medium heat on the stovetop. Toss the pan as they toast, and remove the pan from the heat when they lightly colour and become aromatic.

Put the fennel, cucumber, fennel seeds and chilli in a bowl. Season well and then squeeze over the lemon juice, pour in the olive oil and mix well. In a small bowl, mix the yogurt with the sumac and season with salt and pepper, then add 2 teaspoons of water to thin the yogurt to a dressing consistency.

Place the salad on plates, top with the grilled mackerel and spoon the dressing over and around.

Serves 4

2 small mackerel, pin bones removed
olive oil, for cooking
sea salt and pepper

For the fennel, yogurt and sumac salad
2 tsp fennel seeds
1 large fennel bulb, core removed, very thinly sliced – ideally using a mandoline
⅓ cucumber, finely sliced
1 red chilli, deseeded and finely chopped
juice of ½ lemon
2 Tbsp extra virgin olive oil
3½ Tbsp Greek yogurt
1 tsp sumac

Smoky grilled watermelon with burrata, balsamic and basil

Grilling watermelon over charcoal works surprisingly well. The secret is to get the surface as dry as possible, and this is easily achieved by refrigerating the sliced watermelon, uncovered, for 30–40 minutes. Creamy burrata (cream-filled fresh mozzarella) and some balsamic dressing make this a super-refreshing, healthy dish for the summer months.

Light the barbecue and set for direct cooking.

Cut the watermelon into 4 chunky slices about 2cm (¾in) thick and pat dry with paper towel (the watermelon needs to be sliced this thick to get good caramelization on the grill). Place in the fridge for 30–40 minutes to dry further before grilling.

Place the watermelon slices on the grill in the direct heat zone and cook for 5–6 minutes without turning – you should get a really good, deep colour as the natural sugars caramelize. Turn and cook for 3–4 minutes on the other side, then transfer to a serving plate.

Whisk together the olive oil and balsamic vinegar to make a dressing, then spoon this over the watermelon slices.

Serve with the burrata. Season well with salt and pepper, and finish with a scattering of fresh basil.

Serves 4

½ small watermelon, skin and white pith removed
60ml (4 Tbsp) extra virgin olive oil
20ml (4 tsp) balsamic vinegar
4 burrata, at room temperature
½ bunch basil, leaves picked and roughly torn
sea salt and black pepper

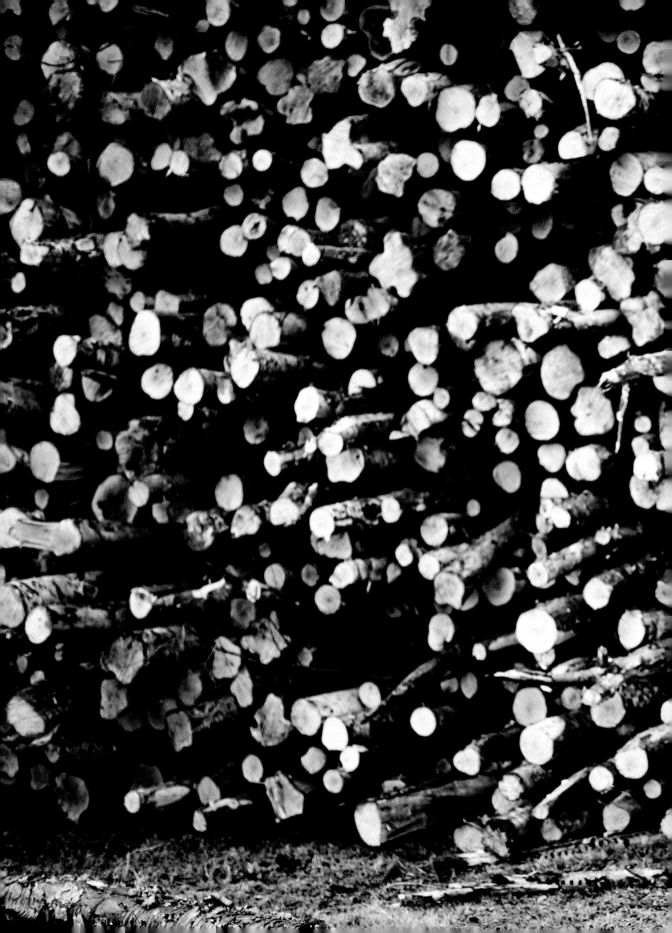

Potato and honey flatbreads with smoked butter and thyme

Our brilliant bakers, Seven Seeded, originally created this flatbread-style recipe for us when we opened Ember Yard, but this version has been tweaked slightly for home baking. Served melting on the bread as it arrives at the table, the smoked butter has become an Ember Yard classic.

You'll need to start the pre-ferment the day before. And if you've got leftover roast potatoes from Sunday lunch to add to the dough, so much the better.

Mix the pre-ferment ingredients together in a bowl, cover and leave at room temperature overnight.

Transfer the pre-ferment to the bowl of a mixer fitted with a dough hook (or a large bowl if making by hand) and add all the remaining ingredients except the semolina flour and sea salt. Start off slowly to bring everything together, then speed up and keep going until everything is fully incorporated. The dough will be very sticky.

Place the dough in a clean bowl and leave in a warm place to prove for an hour or until doubled in size. Knock back the dough, kneading it for 2–3 minutes before returning it to the bowl to prove for another hour.

Remove the dough and divide it in half, then divide each half into 6 balls. Place on a board or tray lined with greaseproof paper and leave at room temperature for 30 minutes. Flatten the balls and shape into flatbreads about 1.5cm (⅝ in) thick, then sprinkle with semolina flour and sea salt. Leave the breads to rest at room temperature for another 30 minutes before cooking.

Light the barbecue and set for direct/indirect cooking. For an extra-smoky flavour, place a lump of wood at the edge of the fire.

Carefully place the flatbreads, 2 or 3 at a time, in the indirect heat zone and close the lid of the barbecue, leaving the vent open. Cook the breads for 6–7 minutes (the temperature inside the barbecue should be about 180°C/350°F), then turn over and cook for a further 4–5 minutes. When they are ready, the breads should be cooked through, crusty and brown.

Serve immediately with smoked butter, thyme and sea salt.

Makes 12 flatbreads

You'll also need a lump of oak or apple wood, if you want an extra-smoky flavour

500g (3⅔ cups) white bread flour
1 tsp dried yeast
3 tsp fine salt
125g (4½oz) roast potatoes, crushed
325ml (3⅓ cups) lukewarm water
1½ Tbsp runny blossom honey
semolina flour and sea salt, for sprinkling
100g (3½oz) Smoked butter (see page 244), thyme leaves and sea salt, to serve

For the pre-ferment
50g (⅓ cup) white bread flour
50 ml (3½ Tbsp) lukewarm water
¾ tsp dried yeast

Grilled sardines on toast with tomatoes and basil

This recipe was inspired by summer jaunts to Spain, and enjoying the simple but sublime *pan con tomate* – bread rubbed with sweet tomatoes. I thought why not add another favourite of mine: smoky, crisp-skinned sardines? They work well together as the tomatoes and basil add a lovely freshness and acidity to the oily fish. I like to serve this with some homemade Alioli (see page 246) on the side.

Light the barbecue and set for direct/indirect cooking.

Drizzle the bread with olive oil and grill on both sides in the direct heat zone until nicely charred. Remove and immediately rub with the crushed garlic cloves and then the halved tomatoes, cut-side down – the idea is to load the bread with the tomato juices and flavour, so a great-tasting tomato is paramount! Place in the indirect heat zone to keep warm.

Season the sliced tomatoes and drizzle with a little oil, then grill in the direct heat zone for a couple of minutes on each side until softened and lightly charred. Move them to the indirect heat zone to keep warm.

Before cooking the sardines, ensure the grill is very clean. Sardine skin is notorious for sticking, so a clean, very hot grill is crucial. Lightly oil the fish, then season and carefully place on the grill, skin-side down. Cook for 2 minutes to char the skin, then carefully turn the fish and finish cooking for a minute on the flesh side. Squeeze over some lemon juice and remove from the grill.

Place the sliced tomatoes on the grilled tomato bread and top with the sardines, finishing with the torn basil leaves.

Serves 4

4 thick slices sourdough bread
2 garlic cloves, lightly crushed
2 very ripe, sweet vine or plum tomatoes, cut in half
2 firm plum tomatoes, cut into thick slices
8 very fresh sardines, butterflied, or 16 sardine fillets
juice of ½ lemon
½ bunch basil, leaves picked and torn
olive oil, for cooking
sea salt and black pepper

Morcilla, apple and potato pancakes

Morcilla is the Spanish version of black pudding. Much softer and creamier, and loaded with smoked paprika, it makes the perfect foil for sharp-sweet apples. Ensure you have a sturdy non-stick frying pan for this, so you can cook and flip the pancakes without any fuss. For something more substantial, add a fried or smoked egg (see page 44) and some grilled pancetta, or freshen things up with a tangle of peppery watercress dressed with a sharp vinaigrette.

Preheat the oven to 180°C (350°F). Scatter a thin layer of salt onto a baking sheet, place the potatoes on top and bake for 1 hour or until the potatoes are soft and tender. Leave to cool before scooping out the flesh into a bowl and discarding the skins.

Light the barbecue and set for direct/indirect cooking.

Place a sauté pan over medium heat on the stovetop. Add the butter, onion, apple and thyme and cook, without colouring, for 3–4 minutes until softened. Transfer to the bowl with the potato flesh, then add the morcilla. Season with the vinegar and some salt and pepper, then mix well and shape into 4 large potato cakes. Chill in the fridge for 20–30 minutes to firm up.

Sit an ovenproof non-stick frying pan on the grill in the direct heat zone of the barbecue and add a lug of olive oil. Carefully place the potato cakes in the pan and fry for 2 minutes on each side to create a crust before moving the pan to the indirect heat zone and closing the lid of the barbecue. Leave to cook for 4–5 minutes until the potato cakes are cooked through and piping-hot. Serve immediately.

Serves 4

about 100g (½ cup) coarse salt
4 medium Desiree potatoes
2 tsp unsalted butter
1 small onion, finely sliced
1 Granny Smith apple, cored, peeled and finely sliced
1 tsp thyme leaves
200g (7oz) morcilla or soft black pudding, skin removed
1 tsp red wine vinegar
sea salt and black pepper
olive oil, for cooking

Fennel and pork sausages with cannellini beans

This is a real hearty breakfast for the cooler months and is inspired by the gutsy, no-holds-barred cooking of Tuscany. You could use any sausage you like here, but pork and fennel is quite an authentic choice and works really well with the rich, tomato-y beans. Grilling the sausages first and then finishing their cooking in the beans not only keeps the sausages plump and moist, but also lets the porky-fennel-infused juices meld with the sauce to create a sublime pot of goodness.

If you are using dried beans, place them in a medium saucepan, cover with fresh water and bring slowly to the boil. Turn down to a simmer and cook for 1–1½ hours until the beans are soft and tender, then drain.

Light the barbecue and set for direct/indirect cooking.

Place a large ovenproof saucepan over the indirect heat zone, add a lug of olive oil and cook the onion and garlic for a couple of minutes to soften. Add the pancetta, fennel seeds and bay leaves and cook for 2 minutes, then tip the beans into the pan, along with the tomatoes. Season well and bring to a simmer.

Meanwhile, place the sausages on the grill in the direct heat zone and cook until nicely browned all over.

Transfer the sausages to the pan of beans and tomatoes, then cover and move it right to the edge of the indirect heat zone and close the lid of the barbecue. Cook slowly for 10–15 minutes until the sausages are cooked through and the tomatoes have reduced to a thick, rich consistency. If the tomatoes seem to be reducing too quickly, just add a little water.

Stir in the parsley, check the seasoning and serve with some crusty bread.

Serves 4

150g (¾ cup) dried cannellini beans, soaked overnight and drained, or 400g (3 cups) cooked cannellini beans, rinsed and drained

1 small onion, finely chopped

2 garlic cloves, finely chopped

50g (1¾oz) smoked pancetta, diced

1 tsp fennel seeds

2 bay leaves

1 x 400g (14½oz) can chopped tomatoes

8 large good-quality pork and fennel sausages

1 small bunch flat-leaf parsley, leaves picked and finely chopped

olive oil, for cooking

sea salt and black pepper

crusty bread, to serve

Flatbreads with anchovy, garlic and rosemary pesto

Brilliant on their own or as part of a feast, these flatbreads couldn't be easier to make. The anchovy isn't overpowering here – it just adds a lovely, intense seasoning. Experiment with different herbs and cheeses once you get going.

Light the barbecue and set for direct/indirect cooking.

Mix the flour, baking powder, yogurt and salt in a bowl until incorporated and then turn out onto a floured surface. Knead the dough for a further 2 minutes, then cover with a plate or cling film and leave for 10 minutes.

To make the pesto, blend all the ingredients to a rough paste in a food processor.

Uncover the dough and divide it in half, then divide each half into 6 balls. Flatten each ball and shape into a rustic flatbread about 12cm (4¾in) in diameter. Score each flatbread a few times with a sharp knife.

Place the rosemary stalks onto the hot coals, then place the flatbreads, 2 or 3 at time, on a hot clean grill in the direct heat zone. Cook for 2 minutes each side until lightly browned and cooked through.

Spoon over the pesto and serve immediately.

Makes 12 small flatbreads

350g (2⅔ cups) self-raising flour
1 tsp baking powder
350g (1½ cups) natural live yogurt
1 tsp fine salt

For the anchovy, garlic and rosemary pesto
8 salted anchovies
3 garlic cloves, finely chopped
1 bunch very fresh rosemary, leaves picked and stalks reserved
40g (½ cup) grated aged pecorino
3 tsp red wine vinegar
100ml (generous ⅓ cup) extra virgin olive oil

Granola with grilled black figs and vanilla-infused buttermilk

You can't beat the freshness and texture of homemade granola, and this combination makes for a delicious all-in-one breakfast. It's best to cook it on the barbecue when the charcoal is low and slow, either after a cooking session or as the barbecue is just getting going, but you could also toast it in the oven. Make a large batch and store it for up to 10 days in a jar.

I like to serve it trifle-style in a glass, with a layer of sticky, grilled figs, then the granola and finally the sweetened, vanilla-infused buttermilk. My wife, Nykeeta, has been honing this granola recipe for over a year and so I really should credit her for it!

Combine the oats and nuts in a large heatproof bowl.

Place the dates, half the honey, the spices and orange zest in a small saucepan and add about a 2cm (¾in) depth of water. Bring to the boil on the stovetop, then simmer for about 12 minutes until the water has reduced by half and the dates are very soft. Blend to a purée with a stick blender or food processor, then add to the oats and nuts, along with the oil. Stir until everything is well coated.

Light the barbecue and set for direct/indirect cooking.

If you're using the barbecue for the granola, you'll need to check the temperature using a probe thermometer or the gauge on the barbecue: you want an internal temperature of about 140–150°C (285–300°F); this will be reached soon after lighting, or while cooling down after cooking. Spread out the oat and nut mixture on a baking sheet and place in the indirect heat zone, then close the lid of the barbecue. Cook for 30 minutes until the granola is dried and golden brown, checking regularly to make sure the nuts don't burn.

If using the oven, preheat it to 175°C (350°F/gas mark 4). Spread out the out and nut mixture on a baking sheet and toast in the oven for 10–15 minutes until golden brown, then reduce the temperature to 110°C (225°F/gas mark ¼) and cook for another 25–30 minutes or until the granola is dried and crispy.

Leave the granola to cool before serving or storing.

To cook the figs, lay them, cut-side down, on the grill in the direct heat zone and cook for 3 minutes before turning and cooking for a further 2 minutes. When they are done, the figs should be lightly charred, soft and jammy.

Mix together the buttermilk with the vanilla seeds and the remaining honey.

To serve, you'll need four glasses, small Kilner-style jars or bowls. Cut each fig half into 3 or 4 pieces and divide between the glasses. Add some of the granola and finish with a spoonful of the buttermilk.

Serves 4

100g (1 cup) jumbo rolled oats
30g (¼ cup) macadamia nuts, roughly chopped
30g (⅓ cup) pecan nuts, roughly chopped
30g (¼ cup) whole hazelnuts
60g (⅓ cup) dried dates, stones removed
4 Tbsp honey
½ tsp mixed spice
½ tsp ground cinnamon
grated zest of ½ orange
2 Tbsp olive oil
4 ripe black figs, cut in half lengthwise
120ml (½ cup) buttermilk
seeds from ½ vanilla pod (bean)

Slow-cooked blackberries with Turkish pide and creamed sheep's cheese

This recipe is inspired by the beautiful breakfasts served in Turkey. Pide is one of my favourite breads to make and eat, as it is light, tasty and cooks very quickly. The creamed sheep's cheese is a revelation; just make sure it's the mildest one you can find (not salty or brined), or use a light goat's curd instead.

Put the blackberries, sugar and lemon juice in a non-reactive saucepan over low heat and cook slowly for about 1 hour until the blackberries have reduced down to a rich, jammy consistency. Remove from the heat and leave to cool.

Whisk together the cheese and cream until smooth. Spoon into a serving bowl and drizzle over the honey, then leave at room temperature to macerate for an hour before serving.

For the pide, combine the flour, yeast, sugar and salt in a bowl. Mix in the water, yogurt and olive oil to make a dough. Cover and leave in a warm place for 1 hour, or until doubled in size.

Light the barbecue and set for direct/indirect cooking.

Line 2 or 3 baking sheets with baking paper and dust lightly with flour. Turn out the dough onto a floured surface, knock it back and then divide into 8. Transfer to the prepared baking sheets and press out to make thin flatbreads roughly 20cm (8in) in diameter. Leave to rest for about 20 minutes before using your fingers to make indentations in the dough (don't press all the way through!).

Lightly brush the breads with yogurt, then carefully transfer the flatbreads to a grill in the direct heat zone. Cook for 2 minutes on each side, or until cooked through and nicely browned.

Serve hot with the slow-cooked blackberries and honey-macerated cheese.

Serves 4–6

500g (3¾ cups) blackberries
150g (¾ cup) caster (superfine) sugar
2 tsp lemon juice
150g (⅔ cup) very mild, soft sheep's cheese
150ml (⅔ cup) double (heavy) cream
200ml (¾ cup) runny honey

For the pide (makes 8)
500g (3⅔ cups) white bread flour, sifted
1 x 7g sachet (2¼ tsp) dried yeast
1 tsp caster (superfine) sugar
2 tsp fine salt
280ml (scant 1¼ cups) lukewarm water
50ml (3½ Tbsp) natural yogurt, plus extra for brushing the breads
2 Tbsp olive oil

TAPAS & SMALL PLATES

Believe it or not, small-plate dining (or *tapas*, to use the Spanish term) isn't a new invention.

You could be forgiven for thinking otherwise, given the recent explosion of restaurants, bars, pubs and books focusing on the concept. So great is the over-exposure that apparently the foodie public and elite gastro-journalists alike are at risk of 'small-plate fatigue' (yes, this term has actually been coined, but I forget by whom), and it often feels as if the whole small-plates-to-share idea is on the cusp of implosion. This reaction has in part been prompted by some ill-conceived efforts: over-complicated and clashing flavours or over-worked dishes that go against the principles of small-plate dining. Dishes should work together in harmony and complement each other, acting as foils to one another and basically making for a delicious experience.

Of course, people all over the world have been eating like this for centuries, and doing it bloody well; the only 'backlash' is in the UK, and more specifically in London, where the culture isn't ingrained. Across much of Asia, including India, Thailand and China, the traditional way of eating is to enjoy many different dishes at the same time: waves of hot and spicy dishes, cooled by fresh salads and sauces, and balanced by rice, noodles and breads. Middle Eastern *mezze* is a perfect example of how a series of simple, well-executed dishes can make a banquet – grilled meat and chicken, flatbreads, pulses, grains and marinated vegetables – all taking into account not only flavours, but also the importance of textures and temperatures, with some dishes served chilled, others warm or piping-hot. And Italy has always had its *antipasti* and *cicchetti*, and, of course, Spain its wonderful *tapas*.

The Spanish *tapas* tradition traces its origins to the pieces of rough, cured ham and dry bread that were used to cover glasses of sweet sherry when not being drunk, to protect the contents from annoying, sugar-loving flies. Eventually, these glass-protectors became bite-sized, salty bar snacks that encouraged lingering... and more drinking. Bar patrons knew they were on to a good thing, and so *tapas* was born. Over the years, the concept has been developed and refined to the point where *tapas* today range from simple salted *padrón* peppers, nuts or olives to salads, grilled fish and meats, slow-cooked braises and crisp-fried croquettes.

We've now been preparing, cooking and serving our own style of *tapas* for over ten years at Salt Yard, and more recently at Dehesa, Opera Tavern and Ember Yard. A direct result of experiencing traditional *tapas* in Spain (and in New York's tapas-style restaurants), this grew from the realization that, done correctly, this is the most wonderful way to eat, creating an informal, relaxed and exciting dining experience – something too many restaurants lack.

We take Spanish and Italian flavours, cooking techniques and ingredients and put our own spin on them. This might be using seasonal, local produce where appropriate: we love using fish from British coastal waters and pork from Gloucester Old Spot pigs; and game and English asparagus feature heavily on our menus during their short seasons. We also make our sauces lighter and fresher, then add a nod to the ever-changing, fast-paced London culinary scene – Ibérico pork and *foie gras* burger, anyone? We always look at the menu as a whole and make sure customers understand what goes with what, and that some things may take a little longer to cook than others, so the meal will have a natural flow. We want our customers to get stuck in and share, to discuss the food they are eating and not be shy about getting a few crumbs on the table.

This kind of eating is about interaction, being social, having fun – and, above all, it's about trying as many different dishes as you can! With a little guidance, there's no reason you can't cook a brilliant tapas feast at home. For each recipe, we've included a couple of suggestions on what we think would complement it, so you can start to build a meal; of course, tastes are subjective, but it will give you an idea. Embrace the small-plate movement, if you haven't already. And if you need a cure for small-plate fatigue, then read on...

These smaller plates are designed for sharing: serve a selection as part of a *tapas* feast; or serve as stand-alone dishes, perhaps as a starter or light lunch.

Each recipe makes 4 individual small plates; if serving *tapas*-style, allow 1 plate between 2 people.

Grilled octopus with mojo verde and peperonata

Octopus has a bit of bad reputation. Tough and chewy are two words that spring to mind – but cooked like this, nothing could be further from the truth. The secret is to buy frozen octopus (or get some fresh octopus and freeze it) from your fishmonger; the thawing process effectively tenderizes the meat. The octopus is then poached before being quickly grilled: simply delicious. Served with some sweet-sour peppers and a piquant green sauce hailing from the Canary Islands, this will transport you to sunny climes. A dollop of Alioli (see page 246) is good with this too.

Dry the octopus with paper towel, then cut off and discard the head. Ensure that the hard beak or mouth has been removed too; this is just at the bottom of the head. Place the octopus in a large saucepan with the white onion, bay leaves and peppercorns, then cover generously with cold water (the octopus will expand as it cooks). Bring to the boil on the stovetop, then turn down to a slow simmer. Cover the pan with a lid or some foil and cook the octopus for around 1 hour, or until very tender – a small knife inserted into the thick part of a tentacle shouldn't meet any resistance. Leave the octopus to cool in the cooking liquid before removing and transferring to the fridge (the poaching liquid makes a delicious soup base).

Light the barbecue and set for direct/indirect cooking.

Place a medium saucepan in the indirect heat zone and pour in a lug of olive oil. Add the red onions and cook slowly, stirring occasionally, until softened. Add the peppers and keep cooking until they are very soft. Now add the vinegar and sugar, season with salt and pepper and cook, stirring occasionally, for about 40 minutes or until the peppers have cooked down to a thick, rich stew. Move the pan to the edge of the barbecue to keep warm.

Separate the tentacles of the octopus. Rub with olive oil and season with salt and pepper, then place them directly on the grill in the direct heat zone and cook for 2 minutes on each side to lightly char.

Spoon out the peperonata, then serve with the grilled octopus and *mojo verde*.

Serve with Paprika-rubbed smoky quails with caramelized onions and alioli (see page 104); Lamb chops with smoky aubergine and salsa verde (see page 73); Smoked and grilled chorizo with roasted peppers and saffron alioli (see page 113)

1 small thawed frozen octopus, about 1–1.5kg (2¼–3½lb) frozen weight
1 white onion, roughly chopped
2 bay leaves
8 black peppercorns
2 red onions, finely sliced
2 red (bell) peppers, deseeded and finely sliced
2 yellow (bell) peppers, deseeded and finely sliced
50ml (3½ Tbsp) red wine vinegar
50g (¼ cup) demerara or brown sugar
olive oil, for cooking
sea salt and black pepper
1 quantity Mojo verde (see page 246)

Young leeks with romesco

Steeped in history, the *Calçotada* is an annual festival that celebrates calçots, a type of large spring onion indigenous to Catalonia. Traditionally, they are cooked over an open fire until blistered and black on the outside and meltingly tender inside. Festival-goers eat them with their bare hands from newspapers, dipping them in romesco sauce as they go. If you can't get your hands on calçots, young leeks make a perfect substitute.

Light and set a barbecue for direct/indirect cooking. Place the wood to the side of the charcoal to start smoking.

Place all the romesco sauce ingredients, except the vinegar and nuts, into a roasting pan and mix well to coat everything in the oil. Cook in the direct heat zone for 5 minutes, then transfer to the indirect heat zone. Close the lid and vent and cook for 40 minutes, stirring occasionally. When ready, the vegetables should be soft and starting to caramelize, and there shouldn't be too much liquid – if there is, move the pan to the direct heat zone and let the liquid reduce for a few minutes. Carefully tip the contents of the roasting pan into a blender. Add the nuts, vinegar and seasoning, then purée until smooth.

Toss the leeks in a little olive oil and season them well. Place directly on the grill in the direct heat zone and cook for 4 minutes on each side until charred on the outside and tender inside. Serve straightaway with the romesco sauce.

Serve with Pinchos morunos (see page 87); Grilled baby artichokes with pine nut purée and poached eggs (page 82)

Serves 4

You'll also need a lump of oak wood

12–16 young leeks, calçots or salad onions
olive oil, for cooking
sea salt and black pepper

For the romesco sauce
½ red onion, diced
1 garlic clove, peeled
½ large red (bell) pepper, deseeded and diced
2 plum tomatoes, diced
½ Tbsp tomato paste
1 red chilli, deseeded and chopped
1 Tbsp smoked hot paprika
2 tsp ground cumin
1½ Tbsp olive oil
1½ Tbsp red wine vinegar
50g (⅓ cup) almonds
50g (⅓ cup) hazelnuts

Lamb chops with smoky aubergine and salsa verde

Lamb features heavily on my menus, whether it's super-sweet and delicate new-season lamb; brinier salt-marsh lamb from sheep grazed near the seashore; or the year-old-plus hoggets that are a little more toothsome but gamier in flavour. Whatever you get, lamb makes the perfect grilling meat. Start this the day before, to give the smoked chops plenty of resting time.

Place the chops in a large non-reactive bowl and pour over the brine, then cover and leave in the fridge for 1 hour.

Set up the cold-smoking device in the barbecue with the wood chips and get it going. Remove the chops from the brine and pat dry with paper towels. Lay them directly on the grill, close the lid of the barbecue and cold-smoke for 1½ hours. Transfer to a clean bowl, cover and leave in the fridge to rest for at least 6 hours, or overnight.

Light the barbecue and set for direct/indirect cooking.

Prick the aubergines with a fork, then cook in the direct heat zone until the skin is blistered and charred all over. Carefully move the aubergines to the indirect heat zone, close the lid of the barbecue and cook for about 1 hour or until the aubergine is soft and has started to collapse. Transfer the aubergines to a bowl. When they are cool enough to handle, remove the stalks, then roughly chop the rest, skin included. Return to the bowl, season with salt and pepper, and stir through the lemon juice. Keep warm.

Place all the salsa verde ingredients in a blender and process to a thick, green purée. Season to taste and reserve.

Season the smoked lamb chops, then place them directly on the grill in the direct heat zone and cook for 3 minutes on each side to caramelize. The lamb will be pink; if you want it well done, cook for a further 2 minutes on each side.

Serve the lamb chops on the chopped aubergine, then spoon over the salsa verde.

Serve with Ibérico presa with jamón butter (see page 84); Grilled fennel with goat's curd, honey and hazelnut picada (see page 94)

Serves 4

You'll also need a cold-smoking device and some oak wood chips

4 large lamb chops or 8 smaller ones
1 quantity Brine for red meat (see page 243)
1 large or 2 medium aubergines (eggplants)
juice of ½ lemon
sea salt and black pepper

For the salsa verde
1 bunch flat-leaf parsley, leaves picked
1 bunch mint, leaves picked
1 bunch basil, leaves picked
3 salted anchovies
1 garlic clove
1 Tbsp capers in brine, drained
100ml (generous ⅓ cup) extra virgin olive oil
1 Tbsp Muscatel vinegar or white balsamic vinegar

Hot-smoked butternut squash with ricotta and grape jam

An unusual but stunning recipe, courtesy of Jacques and Michelle Fourie at Ember Yard. At the restaurant, we bake the squash, then cold-smoke it and finish it over the grill. For home cooking, the hot-smoking process followed by a quick grilling works beautifully. The sweet-sour grape jam and creamy ricotta complement and cool the smokiness.

Light the barbecue and set for direct/indirect cooking. Place the wood to the side of the charcoal to start smoking.

Cut the squash in half lengthwise, scoop out the seeds and then score the flesh in a criss-cross pattern with a sharp knife, being careful not to cut right though. Season with salt and pepper and place on the grill in the indirect heat zone. Close the lid and the vent and cook for about 1½ hours (the temperature inside the barbecue should be 180°C/350°F), throwing a handful of oak chips onto the charcoal halfway through the cooking time.

When the squash is nearly done, put the grapes, sugar, wine and vinegar into a small saucepan. Open the lid of the barbecue, place the pan in the direct heat zone and bring to the boil, then move into the indirect heat zone and simmer for 20 minutes until the grapes have a jammy, syrupy consistency.

The squash is ready when it's nice and tender – the tip of a small knife should go in easily. Cut the squash halves in half lengthwise again, then serve with the ricotta, some grape jam and a sprinkling of oregano leaves.

<u>Serve with</u> Scallops in their shells with wild mushrooms and horseradish gremolata (see page 78); Grilled baby artichokes with pine nut purée and poached eggs (see page 82); Marinated and grilled bavette with smoky salad onions (see page 98)

<u>Serves 4</u>

You'll also need a lump of oak hardwood and some oak wood chips

1 medium butternut squash
500g (3⅓ cups) seedless black grapes
125g (⅔ cup) dark brown sugar
125ml (½ cup) red wine
125ml (½ cup) red wine vinegar
60g (¼ cup) ricotta
1 tsp oregano leaves, to serve
sea salt and black pepper

Scallops in their shells with wild mushrooms and horseradish gremolata

Placed on a hot grill, scallop shells act as a great conductor of heat and smoke, quickly cooking the delicate meat inside to pearly succulence. What's more, you'll have perfect vessels to serve them in! Some might say scallops in the shell are a tad retro, but why would you part them from their natural homes? The earthy mushrooms and punchy horseradish are magic with the scallops.

If you can't find hand-dived scallops with their shells, some plump dredged scallops will suffice – just place them directly onto the grill to cook.

Light and set the barbecue for direct/indirect cooking.

For the horseradish gremolata, mix together the parsley, garlic, horseradish, breadcrumbs, lemon zest and extra virgin olive oil. Season to taste and reserve.

Sort through the wild mushrooms, checking they are nice and clean, before slicing them into thin strips.

Place a frying pan in the direct heat zone and add a lug of olive oil. When the oil is smoking, throw in the mushrooms and sauté until they are cooked through and have started to turn golden brown. Season to taste and add the butter to the pan. When the butter starts foaming, move the pan to the indirect heat zone, squeeze over about half of the lemon juice and keep warm at the edge of the barbecue.

Place the scallop shells on the grill in the direct heat zone and add a little splash of olive oil to each one. When the oil is smoking-hot, add a scallop to each shell and season well. Cook for 2 minutes, then turn the scallops over in the shells, close the lid of the barbecue and cook for another 3 minutes until the scallops are just cooked. Squeeze a little lemon juice on each one.

Serve the scallops in their shells with the buttery wild mushrooms spooned over and a sprinkle of the gremolata.

Serve with Marinated and grilled bavette with smoky salad onions (see page 98); Hot-smoked butternut squash with ricotta and grape jam (see page 74)

Serves 4

120g (4 oz) mixed wild mushrooms
olive oil, for cooking
50g (3½ Tbsp) unsalted butter
juice of 2 lemons
8 large hand-dived scallops, shucked, half-shells reserved
sea salt and black pepper

For the horseradish gremolata
½ bunch flat-leaf parsley, leaves picked and finely chopped
1 garlic clove, finely grated
2 tsp finely grated fresh horseradish
1 Tbsp dried coarse breadcrumbs
finely grated zest of 2 unwaxed lemons
1 Tbsp extra virgin olive oil

Grilled baby artichokes with pine nut purée and poached eggs

Violet baby artichokes are a joy to cook in the spring, and they make the perfect seasonal *tapa*. After we've removed the woody stalk and leaves, we cook them in water, wine and vinegar with plenty of fresh herbs until soft and tender, then grill over hot coals. The pine nut purée is a great thing to have in your armoury – it works wonders with grilled lamb or chicken, and is also delicious eaten as a rich, hummus-like dip. Some beautiful flatbreads would go brilliantly with this.

Trim the ends of the stalks from the artichokes, then keep trimming away the woody, dark-green leaves until you reach the pale-green hearts. With a sharp peeler, peel from the base of the heart to the ends of the stalks, to reveal the tender, pale-green flesh. Use a teaspoon to scrape out the hairy choke, if there is any. Immediately rub the artichokes all over with lemon juice to stop them discolouring, then place in a non-reactive saucepan.

When all the artichokes are prepared, add the wine, vinegar, peppercorns, bay leaf, thyme and a sprinkle of salt to the pan, then pour in enough cold water to cover. Place on the stovetop and bring to the boil, then turn down to a simmer and cook for 12–14 minutes, or until the artichokes are tender (a small knife inserted into the fattest part of the artichoke shouldn't meet any resistance). Drain the artichokes, then leave to cool and dry on paper towel before cutting in half lengthwise.

Light and set a barbecue for indirect/direct cooking.

Place a small frying pan in the indirect heat zone and slowly toast the pine nuts, controlling the heat by moving the pan between heat zones until they have released their natural oils and turned golden brown. Pour in the milk and bring to the boil, then simmer for 3 minutes until the milk has reduced slightly. Pour the pine nuts and milk into a blender, season and process to a smooth purée.

Back on the stovetop, bring a saucepan of water to the boil and add a splash of vinegar. Turn down to a simmer, then carefully slide in the eggs and poach for 3–4 minutes for soft yolks, or 6–7 for more set yolks. Lift out with a slotted spoon and drain well.

While the eggs are poaching, lightly drizzle the artichokes with olive oil and season them. Lay them on the grill in the direct heat zone and cook for 2–3 minutes on each side until lightly charred.

Serve the grilled artichokes alongside the pine nut purée and finish with the poached eggs.

Serve with Young leeks with romesco (see page 72)

Serves 4

4 small artichokes or 8 baby violet artichokes

juice of ½ lemon

300ml (1¼ cups) white wine

300ml (1¼ cups) white wine vinegar, plus a splash extra

5 black peppercorns

1 bay leaf

1 sprig thyme

65g (½ cup) pine nuts

175ml (¾ cup) full-cream (whole) milk

4 free-range eggs, each cracked into a cup

olive oil, for cooking

sea salt and black pepper

Ibérico presa with jamón butter

This is another Ember Yard classic. Now relatively easy to get hold of, Ibérico pork's incredible fat marbling and sweet-nutty flavour is largely due to the pigs' foraged diet, which includes woodland acorns. Their meat is best cooked to medium-rare, just as you would for beef. If you can't get Ibérico pork, I'd suggest beef rib eye as an alternative.

This whipped jamón butter is super-versatile. We've even been known to spread it thickly on toast for a naughty, indulgent late-night treat.

Place the steaks in a bowl with the blackening rub and massage into the meat. Drizzle over the honey and lightly massage again until the meat is fully coated. Cover and leave to marinate in the fridge for 1½ hours.

For the jamón butter, place a small frying pan over medium heat on the stovetop. Add the jamón and gently sauté for 2–3 minutes to lightly caramelize and release its natural fats. Remove from the heat and allow to cool slightly before mixing with the soft butter and seasoning with a little salt (remember the ham is salty). When fully incorporated, cover and leave at cool room temperature.

Light the barbecue and set for direct/indirect cooking.

Take the meat out of the fridge 10 minutes before cooking, to bring it to room temperature.

Throw the thyme stalks onto the charcoal. Season the steaks with salt, then place them on the grill in the direct heat zone. Close the lid of the barbecue and leave the steaks for 4 minutes to caramelize and 'blacken' before turning over and cooking for a further 4 minutes, still with the lid closed – the meat should be medium-rare. Move the steaks to the edge of the barbecue and leave to rest for 3 minutes, then squeeze over some lemon juice.

Cut the meat into thick slices and serve with the jamón butter on the side.

Serve with Lamb chops with smoky aubergine and salsa verde (see page 73)

Serves 4

2 x 200g (7oz) steaks of Ibérico presa (shoulder) or beef rib eye
2 tsp Blackening rub (see page 243)
1 Tbsp runny honey
small handful of thyme stalks
juice of ½ lemon
sea salt and black pepper

For the jamón butter
25g (1 oz) jamón Ibérico, Serrano ham or prosciutto, finely diced
150g (⅔ cup) unsalted butter, at room temperature

Thyme-smoked mussels with samphire, fino and chilli

Choose large, plump mussels for this and make sure they are all tightly closed when you buy them. Then it couldn't be simpler: just throw the mussels on a nice hot barbecue and close the lid. As soon as they open they are ready, and they will have taken on the smokiness of the coals. I like to sprinkle the thyme stalks on the charcoal for an extra burst of flavour as well.

Wash the mussels in running cold water for 30 minutes.

Light and set a barbecue for direct cooking.

Pour the sherry into a small saucepan and reduce by half on the stovetop, then whisk in the butter and reserve.

Drain the mussels thoroughly and check them over, discarding any broken or open shells, then place in a bowl and toss with a little olive oil.

Scatter the thyme stalks onto the hot charcoal. Throw the mussels on the barbecue – watch out for flames – and use long-handled tongs to spread them out into one even layer. Close the lid of the barbecue and cook for 6–7 minutes or until the mussels have opened, then immediately transfer to a large bowl and add the sherry butter, chilli, samphire, thyme, lemon juice and some pepper. Cover the bowl and leave for 2 minutes, shaking once or twice to make sure everything is mixed well together and the samphire gets lightly steamed.

Divide the mussels and samphire evenly between the plates, pouring over any juices that have collected in the bottom of the bowl.

Serve with Chilli-spiked grilled mackerel with lemon pickle, young spinach and sumac (see page 95); Grilled fennel with goat's curd, honey and hazelnut picada (see page 94); Grilled baby artichokes with pine nut purée and poached eggs (see page 82); Scallops in their shells with wild mushrooms and horseradish gremolata (see page 78)

Serves 4

1kg (2¼lb) large mussels, scrubbed and debearded

375ml (1⅔ cups) fino, or other very dry sherry

50g (3½ Tbsp) unsalted butter

1 small bunch thyme, leaves picked and stalks reserved

2 red chillies, deseeded and finely chopped

100g (3½oz) samphire

juice of ½ lemon

olive oil, for cooking

black pepper

Pinchos morunos

Popular across the Spanish regions of Andalucia and Extremadura, these marinated meat skewers trace their origins to the Moorish occupation of Spain, the cumin and coriander telltale signs of an exotic influence. They are fantastic grilled over charcoal or wood, as the spicy meat really benefits from the lick of an open flame. We make these with Ibérico pork, but you could use lamb leg, a fattier cut of beef such as rib eye, or rare-breed British pork like Gloucester Old Spot. These are delicious with Mojo verde (see page 246).

Cut the pork into 2cm (¾in) cubes, then thread onto four metal kebab skewers, dividing the meat evenly between them.

Place the meat skewers on a tray or plate. Season well, then sprinkle over the paprika, cumin, coriander, vinegar and oil. Mix well, massaging the spices into the meat, then leave to marinade in the fridge for at least 2 hours.

Light and set the barbecue for direct/indirect cooking.

Drain the marinade off the pork, then place the skewers on the grill in the direct heat zone and cook for 2 minutes on each side until the meat is nicely charred and just cooked – make sure it's still slightly pink in the middle, so it will be juicy. Move to a warm spot to rest for 2 minutes and then squeeze over the lemon juice just before serving.

Serve with Young leeks with romesco (see page 72)

Serves 4

You'll also need four metal kebab skewers

400g (14oz) pork loin, either Ibérico or British rare-breed
2 Tbsp smoked paprika
2 Tbsp ground cumin
1 tsp coriander seeds, crushed
1½ Tbsp red wine vinegar
100ml (generous ⅓ cup) extra virgin olive oil
juice of ½ lemon
sea salt and black pepper

Chargrilled duck breast with peas, broad beans and hot mint sauce

I love cooking this dish in early summer, when peas and beans are at their sweetest and most vibrant; however, for convenience or out of season, you can use good-quality frozen peas and beans. As well as adding extra flavour, brining the duck breast beforehand helps to keep it succulent. To get the skin nice and crisp, it's best to score it and render the fat over a low heat, then you can ramp up the fire to cook the meat quickly so it stays pink. The hot mint sauce has an exotic North-African edge to it that works well with fatty meats – the acidity of the hot vinegar cuts through the richness.

Trim the duck breasts of any excess fat and sinew, then use a very sharp knife to lightly score the skin in a criss-cross pattern, without cutting into the flesh. Put in a non-reactive bowl, pour over the brine and refrigerate to cure for 1 hour.

For the hot mint sauce, place the extra virgin olive oil, garlic, mint stalks and the cumin and coriander seeds in a small, non-reactive saucepan and place over medium heat on the stovetop. When the garlic starts to turn golden, remove the pan from the heat and carefully pour in the vinegar. Season well, then set aside for an hour or so to infuse.

If you are using fresh peas and beans, cook them in boiling salted water for 2 minutes. Refresh in iced water, then drain.

Light the barbecue and set for direct/indirect cooking.

Remove the duck breasts from the brine and pat dry with a paper towel. Place the duck, skin-side down, on the grill in the indirect heat zone and throw a small handful of cherry wood chips onto the charcoal. Close the lid of the barbecue and cook the duck for 4 minutes to render some of the fat and lightly caramelize the skin. Open the lid, transfer the duck to the direct cooking zone, throw another small handful of wood chips onto the charcoal and close the lid. Cook for 5–6 minutes, still skin-side down, then turn the duck breasts onto the flesh side and cook for 2 minutes or until cooked to medium (if you press your finger into the meat, it should bounce back); give it another 3–4 minutes if you want it well done. Move the duck to a warm spot to rest for 5 minutes.

Strain the infused mint sauce into a clean saucepan, then add the peas and broad beans and bring to the boil in the direct heat zone. Season the sauce well, throw in the mint leaves and remove from the heat as soon as the mint has wilted.

Spoon some of the peas and beans onto the plate, then thickly slice the duck breasts and place on top. Spoon over the rest of the peas and beans, drizzle over the hot mint sauce and serve.

Serve with Grilled fennel with goat's curd, honey and hazelnut picada (see page 94); Lamb chops with smoky aubergine and salsa verde (see page 73)

Serves 4

You'll also need some cherry wood chips

- 2 x 200g (7oz) Gressingham or Barbary duck breasts
- ½ quantity Brine for red meat (see page 243)
- 70g (½ cup) fresh or thawed frozen peas
- 70g (⅔ cup) fresh or thawed frozen broad beans, outer skins removed
- sea salt and black pepper

For the hot mint sauce
- 75ml (⅓ cup) extra virgin olive oil
- 1 large garlic clove, thinly sliced
- 1 bunch mint, stalks and leaves separated
- 1 tsp cumin seeds
- 1 tsp coriander seeds, lightly crushed
- 50ml (3½ Tbsp) Cabernet Sauvignon vinegar or other red wine vinegar

Beetroot with blood orange, almonds and chard

By far the best way to cook beetroot is to wrap them in foil and bake them very slowly in the dying embers of the charcoal. I often put some in at the end of a cooking session and leave them overnight, in the morning you'll have some super-tender, sweet, delicious beets, or pop them in the coals at the start of cooking and they'll be ready in a couple of hours. This is the ideal dish to cook in the background while you're cooking your other stuff.

Wash the beetroot and trim off any leaves. Wrap each beetroot in foil, adding a sprinkle of salt and a splash of vinegar to each parcel before sealing.

Light the barbecue and set for direct/indirect cooking.

Using long-handled tongs, you can either bury your beetroot parcels among the coals when they reach optimum cooking temperature, or at the end of a cooking session when the embers are dying down. Just make sure the parcels are surrounded by coals and nestle them in well, so they cook properly. They will take around 2 hours to cook through; check by inserting the tip of a small knife into the centre – it shouldn't meet any resistance. Once they're done, let them cool slightly before unwrapping the foil and peeling off the skin while the beetroot is still warm.

Slice the beetroot and place in a bowl, along with the remaining vinegar and the extra virgin olive oil. Season with salt and pepper.

Use a sharp knife to cut away the skin and pith of the oranges, then slice into rounds and reserve.

Place a frying pan over medium heat on the stovetop. Add a splash of olive oil, followed by the chilli, chard and some salt and pepper. Cook briefly for 2 minutes, just until the chard has wilted, then transfer to the bowl with the beetroot and toss through well.

Divide the beetroot and chard evenly between four plates, then top with orange slices and scatter over the almonds.

<u>Serve with</u> Chilli-spiked grilled mackerel with lemon pickle, young spinach and sumac (see page 95); Paprika-rubbed smoky quails with caramelized onions and alioli (see page 104); Ember Yard smoked burger with smoked Spanish cheese (see page 114); Marinated and grilled bavette with smoky salad onions (see page 98)

<u>Serves 4</u>

1kg (2¼lb) small beetroot (beets) – a selection of red, yellow and candy is nice

50ml (3½ Tbsp) Cabernet Sauvignon vinegar or other red wine vinegar

50ml (3½ Tbsp) extra virgin olive oil

2 blood oranges or 1 regular orange

1 red chilli, deseeded and thinly sliced

100g (3½oz) baby chard, collard greens or other seasonal leafy greens

handful of Marcona almonds or blanched, salted almonds, roughly chopped

olive oil, for cooking

sea salt and black pepper

Grilled fennel with goat's curd, honey and hazelnut picada

As these thick slices of fennel soften and char on the grill, their natural juices are concentrated and caramelized, with delicious results. Picada is a North-African kitchen stalwart; it can be used to thicken stews and sauces, or to add an interesting, crunchy element to a dish, as I've done here.

Light the barbecue and set for direct/indirect cooking.

Trim the fennel bulbs and cut them into thick slices lengthwise. Season the fennel slices and drizzle them with olive oil, then lay them on the grill in the direct heat zone. Grill for 2 minutes on each side to char, then move to the indirect heat zone and close the lid of the barbecue. Cook for 7 minutes before turning the fennel and cooking for a further 5 minutes until it is very tender and nicely charred. When the fennel is done, move it to the edge of the barbecue to keep warm while you make the picada.

Place a frying pan in the direct heat zone and add a good lug of olive oil. Rip the bread into small pieces and throw into the pan. Season well and fry until the bread turns a light golden brown before adding the hazelnuts. Cook for 3–4 minutes until both the bread and the nuts are a deep golden brown, moving the pan from direct to indirect heat as needed, so the nuts don't burn. Transfer the nuts and bread to a bowl and add the vinegar and extra virgin olive oil. Using a potato masher or the back of a spoon, roughly crush the bread and nuts into the oil and vinegar to make a rough, loose paste.

Place the grilled fennel on plates, spoon over the picada and drizzle with honey, then serve with the goat's curd on the side.

Serve with Chilli-spiked grilled mackerel with lemon pickle, young spinach and sumac (see page 95); Cuttlefish with squash, nduja and marjoram (see page 96); Smoked cod with white beans, clams and parsley (see page 110); Lamb chops with smoky aubergine and salsa verde (see page 73)

Serves 4

2 medium fennel bulbs

olive oil, for cooking

1 slice of day-old bread, crusts removed

50g (⅓ cup) hazelnuts, roughly chopped

2 Tbsp red wine vinegar

2 Tbsp extra virgin olive oil

2 Tbsp runny blossom honey

125g (4oz) goat's curd or very mild, soft goat's cheese

sea salt and black pepper

Chilli-spiked grilled mackerel with lemon pickle, young spinach and sumac

In various guises, this dish has served us well over the years. Like many other oily fish, mackerel works brilliantly over a grill as the natural oils lubricate the flesh as it cooks. The lemon pickle is one of my favourite condiments, relying solely on beautiful-quality lemons. It's so easy to make – and the remainder will last in the fridge for a good couple of weeks, ready to serve with any grilled or roasted meat or fish.

First make the pickle. Place the lemons, sugar and extra virgin olive oil in a blender, blitz to a purée and then quickly blend in the marjoram or oregano. Season to taste with salt and pepper, adding a little more sugar if you'd like it sweeter.

Light the barbecue and set for direct/indirect cooking.

Throw the reserved herb stalks onto the charcoal. Rub the mackerel with olive oil and season all over with salt and pepper and the chilli flakes. Like sardines, the skin on mackerel is quite delicate, so make sure your grill is clean and hot to help avoid sticking. Lay the fish on a clean grill in the indirect heat zone. Cook for 4 minutes on each side, or until the skin is crispy and charred and the flesh is starting to become opaque. Mackerel benefits from being left a little pink in the middle. Remove the mackerel from the grill, squeeze over some lemon juice and leave to rest while you prepare the spinach.

Place a medium saucepan in the direct heat zone. Add a lug of olive oil and the baby spinach leaves. Season and cook, stirring, until just wilted.

Serve the mackerel on a bed of spinach with the lemon pickle on the side. Sprinkle with the sumac and some more fresh marjoram leaves, if you like.

Serve with Beetroot with blood orange, almonds and chard (see page 92); Smoked cod with white beans, clams and parsley (see page 110)

Serves 4

2 unwaxed organic lemons (Amalfi are wonderful, if they're in season), cut into quarters and seeds removed
about 2 Tbsp caster (superfine) sugar
100ml (generous ⅓ cup) extra virgin olive oil
1 Tbsp marjoram or oregano leaves, stalks reserved
2 small mackerel, pin-boned and skin lightly scored
¼ tsp dried chilli flakes
juice of ½ lemon
2 handfuls baby spinach leaves
¼ tsp sumac
olive oil, for cooking
sea salt and black pepper

Cuttlefish with squash, nduja and marjoram

Cuttlefish is relatively under-used in the UK, which is a real shame. Similar to squid, but perhaps a little more toothsome and with a richer, deeper flavour, it's equally good cooked quickly over a high heat or slowly braised in a stew. The Spaniards eat cuttlefish by the bucket-load... and they know their seafood. Ask your fishmonger to get some cuttlefish for you, and to clean it, separating the head and body – they're usually delighted to help. Failing that, some meaty, fresh squid will do the trick. Sweet squash, fiery nduja and herby marjoram complete the package here, making an excellent dish.

Remove any seeds from the squash, then cut it into quarters lengthwise.

Light the barbecue and set for direct/indirect cooking.

Rub the squash with olive oil and season, then place directly on the grill in the direct heat zone and cook for 2 minutes on each side to lightly char. Transfer to the indirect heat zone, close the lid of the barbecue and cook for 25–30 minutes, checking and turning it every now and again until the squash is soft and tender.

Meanwhile, slowly heat the nduja in a small saucepan with a splash of water on the stovetop until it has just melted into a thick sauce. Keep warm.

When the squash is done, move it to the edge of the barbecue to keep warm. Check the charcoal is hot enough (it needs to be very hot to quickly sear the cuttlefish); if not, add a little more charcoal.

Cut the cuttlefish into chunks, drizzle with olive oil and season well. Place the cuttlefish directly on the grill in the direct zone and cook quickly for 2 minutes on each side to lightly char. Don't cook for any longer, or it will become chewy.

Squeeze some lemon juice over the cuttlefish, then serve with the squash, some nduja sauce and a sprinkling of marjoram.

Serve with Grilled fennel with goat's curd, honey and hazelnut picada (see page 94); Slow-cooked chicken legs with polenta, gorgonzola and oregano (see page 106)

<u>Serves 4</u>

½ butternut squash
50g (2oz) nduja or soft, spicy chorizo, skin removed
240g (8½oz) cuttlefish or squid, cleaned
juice of ½ lemon
small handful of marjoram leaves
olive oil, for cooking
sea salt and black pepper

Marinated and grilled beef bavette with smoky salad onions

I find bavette to be one of the tastiest cuts of beef around. Cut from the animal's strong, well-exercised abdominal muscles, the meat should be sliced against the grain to maximize tenderness; a little brining also helps. Don't expect melt-in-the-mouth fillet here, though. This is beef that needs a little chewing, but the flavour more than makes up for that, and the smoky onions and zingy-crunchy salsa are the perfect accompaniments. Delicious.

Place the beef in the brine and leave, covered, for 1 hour. Drain and transfer to a clean bowl. Add the extra virgin olive oil, garlic, chilli, lemon zest and thyme, then leave to marinate for at least 1 hour.

Light the barbecue and set for direct/indirect cooking.

Remove the beef from the marinade, season with salt and pepper and place on the grill in the direct heat zone. Keep a close eye on the steaks: bavette cooks quickly as it is quite thin, and it shouldn't be cooked past medium-rare otherwise it'll be tough. Grill for 2 minutes on each side to char, then move to the cooler edge of the barbecue to rest for a couple of minutes.

Cut the onions in half lengthwise, keeping the stalks intact. Toss them with a little olive oil, season with salt and pepper and place directly on the grill in the direct heat zone and cook for 3–4 minutes until charred and tender.

Thickly slice the steaks and serve with the grilled onions and salsa cruda.

Serve with Slow-cooked chicken legs with polenta, gorgonzola and oregano (see page 106); Beetroot with blood orange, almonds and chard (see page 92)

Serves 4

4 x 100g (3½oz) pieces of beef bavette, onglet or thinly sliced rump

1 quantity Brine for red meat (see page 243)

100ml (generous ⅓ cup) extra virgin olive oil

2 garlic cloves, roughly chopped

1 small red chilli, deseeded and finely chopped

finely grated zest of 1 lemon

1 tsp thyme leaves

8 large salad onions or large, bulbous spring onions

1 quantity Crunchy shallot and garlic salsa cruda (see page 247)

olive oil, for cooking

sea salt and black pepper

Cold-smoked sea bream with pomegranate, bottarga and coriander

This is a beautiful, light dish that's perfect for a summer's evening. The bream is simply cured and then delicately cold-smoked with apple wood chips to add a subtle fragrance, rather than a full-on smoked salmon effect! Just remember to allow time for the fish to rest after smoking – it needs at least 6 hours.

The Sardinian speciality of bottarga is cured and air-dried mullet roe. Incredibly delicious, it is well worth seeking out, but if you can't find it, salted and dried anchovies will give you a similar briny-umami hit.

Place the fish on a tray or plate and scatter over the dry cure. Ensure the fish is coated all over with the cure, then cover and leave in the fridge for 1 hour.

Set up the cold-smoking device in the barbecue with the wood chips and get it going.

Remove the fish and rinse very briefly under cold water to remove any excess cure, then pat dry with a paper towel. Place the fillets, skin-side down, on the grill, then close the lid and vent of the barbecue. Cold-smoke for about 1½ hours – the fish should take on a pale yellow hue. Transfer the smoked fish to a clean tray or plate, cover and leave in the fridge to rest for at least 6 hours, or overnight.

To serve, finely slice the fish slices with a long, sharp knife, discarding the skin

Divide the fish slices between plates, season well and drizzle with olive oil.

Remove the seeds from the pomegranate, working over a bowl to collect any juices. Dot the pomegranate seeds around the fish, pouring over any juices, then finish with coriander leaves and bottarga or anchovies. Serve immediately.

Serve with Paprika-rubbed smoky quails with caramelized onions and alioli (see page 104); Grilled fennel with goat's curd, honey and hazelnut picada (see page 94); Grilled baby artichokes with pine nut purée and poached eggs (page 82)

Serves 4

You'll also need a cold-smoking device and some apple wood chips

2 large (each 180g [6oz]) fillets of very fresh sea bream

30g (2 Tbsp) Dry fish cure (see page 242)

½ pomegranate (or 1 blood orange when in season)

small handful of coriander (cilantro) leaves

½ tsp grated bottarga or ½ tsp finely chopped dried anchovies

extra virgin olive, for drizzling

sea salt and black pepper

Paprika-rubbed smoky quails with caramelized onions and alioli

Quails make a perfect little *tapa* and are becoming readily available in the UK. Go to any bar in Spain and you'll likely find quails with garlic and oil on the menu – they're as ubiquitous as chorizo and anchovies. For this recipe, I've brined the quails first to help them stay moist and plump on the grill and then spatchcocked them so they cook quickly and evenly. Don't forget to allow time for the quails to rest after cold-smoking; they need at least 6 hours, but can be left overnight if that's more convenient.

Place the quails in a non-reactive bowl and pour over the brine. Cover and leave in the fridge for 1 hour, then drain and pat dry with a paper towel.

Set up the cold-smoking device in the barbecue with the wood chips and get it going. Lay the quails, skin-side up, on the grill, then close the lid and vent of the barbecue and cold-smoke for 2 hours. Transfer the quails to a clean tray or plate, cover and leave in the fridge to rest for at least 6 hours or overnight.

Light the barbecue and set for direct/indirect cooking.

Place a medium saucepan in the indirect heat zone, then add a lug of olive oil, along with the onions and sugar. Cook slowly for 1 hour, stirring occasionally and varying the heat as necessary, until soft and lightly caramelized. When the onions are done, move the pan to the edge of the barbecue to keep warm.

Rub the quails with olive oil, season and then rub them with smoked paprika. Lay the quails, skin-side down, on the grill in the direct heat zone and cook for 3 minutes until the skin starts to crisp and lightly char. Turn over and cook for a further 3 minutes, then move to the indirect heat zone and rest for 2 minutes. The quail meat should still be slightly pink.

Squeeze over some lemon juice, then cut each quail in half lengthwise. Serve with the caramelized onions and a dollop of alioli.

Serve with Smoked and grilled chorizo with roasted peppers and saffron alioli (see page 113); Cold-smoked sea bream with pomegranate, bottarga and coriander (see page 102)

Serves 4

You'll also need a cold-smoking device and some oak wood chips

2 large quails, spatchcocked – ask your butcher to do this for you
1 quantity Brine for white meat (see page 243)
3 medium onions, finely sliced
2 tsp dark brown sugar
2 Tbsp smoked hot paprika
juice of ½ lemon
olive oil, for cooking
sea salt and black pepper
1 quantity Alioli (see page 246), to serve

Slow-cooked chicken legs with polenta, gorgonzola and oregano

A great autumn *tapa*: free-range chicken legs cooked long and slow, so the skin is burnished and crisp, and the meat is soft and tender with a delicate smokiness. Delicious with some warming, creamy polenta infused with blue cheese.

Place the chicken in a large bowl and pour over the brine, then cover and leave in the fridge for 1 hour.

Light and set the barbecue for direct/indirect cooking. Place the wood to the side of the charcoal.

Remove the chicken legs from the brine and pat dry with a paper towel. Place them, skin-side down, on the grill in the direct heat zone and cook for 2 minutes, just to start caramelizing the skin. Transfer the chicken legs to the indirect heat zone, still skin-side down, and close the lid of the barbecue (the temperature inside the barbecue should be 180°C/350°F). Cook for 1–1¼ hours or until the skin is crisp and deep brown, the meat is very tender and the juices run clear.

About 20 minutes before the chicken should be ready, pour the milk into a saucepan and bring to the boil on the stovetop. Add the butter and whisk until melted, then whisk in the polenta. Continue to whisk until the polenta is fully incorporated, then turn down the heat to a simmer and cook slowly for 5–6 minutes, depending on the brand. The polenta should be quite thick, smooth and not grainy. Finally, whisk in the parmesan and gorgonzola and season to taste.

Divide the polenta evenly between warmed bowls, top with a chicken leg and serve sprinkled with oregano leaves.

<u>Serve with</u> Smoked cod with white beans, clams and parsley (see page 110); Marinated and grilled bavette with smoky salad onions (see page 98); Beetroot with blood orange, almonds and chard (see page 92); Cuttlefish with squash, nduja and marjoram (see page 96)

Serves 4

You'll also need a lump of oak wood

4 small free-range chicken legs

1 quantity Brine for white meat (see page 243)

500ml (generous 2 cups) full-cream (whole) milk

30g (2 Tbsp) unsalted butter

90g (⅔ cup) instant polenta (cornmeal)

50g (¾ cup) finely grated parmesan

50g (½ cup) crumbled gorgonzola

2 tsp oregano leaves, to serve

sea salt and black pepper

Smoked cod with white beans, clams and parsley

Here we salt-cure the cod before cold-smoking it with oak chips. The cod is then grilled to smoky deliciousness. This dish was inspired by the cuisine of the Spanish Basque Country, where cod, parsley and clams are considered the holy trinity of the gastronomic world.

Place the cod on a tray or plate and scatter over the dry cure. Ensure the fish is coated all over with the cure, then cover and leave in the fridge for 1 hour.

Set up the cold-smoking device in the barbecue with the wood chips and get it going. Remove the cod and rinse very briefly under cold water to remove any excess cure. Place the fillets, skin-side down, on the grill, then close the lid and vent of the barbecue and cold-smoke for 1 hour and 20 minutes. Transfer the smoked cod to a clean tray or plate, cover and leave in the fridge to rest for at least 6 hours, or overnight.

If you are using dried white beans, cook them in simmering unsalted water for about 1½ hours or until tender, then drain well and reserve.

Light and set the barbecue for direct/indirect cooking.

Place a medium saucepan in the direct heat zone and add a lug of olive oil. Add the shallot and garlic and cook gently, without colouring, until soft (you may need to move the pan into the indirect zone to regulate the heat). Pour in the cider, then tip in the clams. Cover the pan and steam until the clams open, discarding any that don't. Use a slotted spoon to transfer the clams to a bowl, leaving the cider and cooking liquid in the pan. Add the beans to the pan, along with the butter and parsley, and leave to simmer gently while you cook the cod.

Season the smoked cod fillets and brush with olive oil, then place them, skin-side down, on the grill. Cook for 2–3 minutes on each side, depending on the thickness of the fillets. When it is done, the flesh should be opaque with a nicely charred and caramelized exterior. Squeeze over some lemon juice.

Tip the clams back into the pan with the beans to heat through. Check the seasoning and add a squeeze of lemon juice, if it needs it, then divide the beans and clams evenly between the plates. Sit the cod on top and serve.

Serve with Chilli-spiked grilled mackerel with lemon pickle, young spinach and sumac (see page 95); Slow-cooked chicken legs with polenta, gorgonzola and oregano (see page 106)

Serves 4

You'll also need a cold-smoking device and some fine oak wood chips

4 x 100g (3½oz) fillets of cod, skin on

40g (3 Tbsp) Dry fish cure (see page 242)

200g (1¼ cups) dried white beans, soaked overnight, or 400g (2½ cups) good-quality, cooked white beans, rinsed and drained

1 large shallot, finely sliced

1 garlic clove, chopped

100ml (generous ⅓ cup) dry cider

200g (7oz) clams in the shell, scrubbed

50g (3½ Tbsp) unsalted butter

1 small bunch flat-leaf parsley, roughly chopped

juice of ½ lemon

olive oil, for cooking

sea salt and black pepper

Smoked and grilled chorizo with roasted peppers and saffron alioli

You can buy ready-smoked chorizo, but I prefer to cold-smoke fresh cooking chorizo with apple wood chips and then grill it quickly over a high heat. There's nothing quite like the smell of grilling chorizo for causing a stir and an impromptu gathering around the grill! A cooling saffron alioli is just the thing for dipping the hot chorizo, and the vivid yellow looks great with the paprika-red meat.

Set up the cold-smoking device in the barbecue with the wood chips and get it going.

Place the chorizo on the grill, then close the lid and vent of the barbecue and cold-smoke for 2 hours. Transfer the smoked chorizo to a tray or plate, cover and leave in the fridge to rest for at least 6 hours, or overnight.

Set and light the barbecue for direct/indirect cooking.

Place the peppers directly onto the grill in the direct heat zone and grill on all sides to blacken. Transfer the peppers to the indirect heat zone, close the lid of the barbecue and cook for 20 minutes or until the peppers are soft and have started to collapse. Place the peppers in a heatproof bowl and cover with cling film while they are still hot. Leave to steam for 15 minutes, then peel off the skins and remove any seeds.

Roughly slice the peppers, then place in a clean bowl, along with the garlic, thyme, extra virgin olive oil, vinegar and seasoning. Set aside to marinate for 15 minutes before you start to grill the smoked chorizo.

Cut the chorizo in half lengthwise, place on the grill in the direct heat zone and cook for 2 minutes on each side until lightly charred and cooked through.

Whisk the saffron-infused water into the alioli. Spoon the marinated peppers onto the plates, then serve with the hot-grilled chorizo and a dollop of the alioli.

Serve with Grilled octopus with mojo verde and peperonata (see page 71); Paprika-rubbed smoky quails with caramelized onions and alioli (see page 104)

Serves 4

You'll also need a cold-smoking device and some apple wood chips

350g (12oz) soft, spicy cooking chorizo (about 6 sausages), peeled

1 large red (bell) pepper

1 large yellow (bell) pepper

1 garlic clove, finely chopped

1 tsp thyme leaves

50ml (3½ Tbsp) extra virgin olive oil

50ml (3½ Tbsp) white balsamic vinegar

2 pinches of saffron strands, infused in a splash of warm water

sea salt and black pepper

1 quantity Alioli (see page 246), to serve

Ember Yard smoked burger with smoked Spanish cheese

Since we do tapas at Salt Yard Group, I never thought we'd become known for our burgers. But times change, and now we've got two hits under our belt: the Opera Tavern's Ibérico pork and *foie gras* burger, and this one from Ember Yard – which is not just any old burger, as you'll see. We decided to cold-smoke the beef rump before grinding it with some lardo (pork back fat) and shaping it into burgers. Topped with the smoked Basque sheep's cheese called Idiazabel, and served with lashings of alioli and chorizo ketchup, it's been such a success that we daren't take it off the menu.

Set up the cold-smoking device in the barbecue with the wood chips and get it going.

Spread out the mince on a small baking sheet. Place in the barbecue, close the lid and vent and cold-smoke for 1½ hours. Remove the smoked mince from the barbecue, cover and leave in the fridge to rest for at least 6 hours, or overnight.

Light and set a barbecue for direct/indirect cooking.

Transfer the smoked mince to a bowl and add the shallot, breadcrumbs, milk and plenty of seasoning. Grate the frozen lardo or pancetta directly into the mince, then mix everything together very well. Before shaping the burgers, I like to fry off a little bit of the mince mixture to check the seasoning. Taste and adjust as necessary, then divide the mince into quarters and use your hands to mould into four burgers.

Place the burgers on the grill in the direct heat zone and cook for 2 minutes on each side to lightly char, then transfer to the indirect heat zone. Sprinkle a quarter of the cheese on top of each burger, then close the lid and leave for 5 minutes until the cheese has melted and the burgers are cooked to medium (good mince can happily be left a little pink). To check if they're done, press one with your finger – the meat should spring back into shape. Rest the burgers in a warm spot for a couple of minutes while you get everything else ready.

Cut the burger buns and quickly grill the cut side to add a little char. Spoon some alioli on the base of each bun, followed by a lettuce leaf, a spoonful of the ketchup, then a burger, some red onion slices and the top of the bun. For a natty, restaurant-style presentation, spear a guindilla pepper or green chilli onto a skewer, then push the skewer right through the burger. A crowd-pleaser, if ever there was one!

<u>Serve with</u> Beetroot with blood orange, almonds and chard (see page 92); Ibérico presa with jamón butter (see page 84)

Serves 4

You'll also need a cold-smoking device and some fine oak wood chips

400g (14oz) good-quality minced beef (ideally aged rump, freshly minced – ask your butcher nicely)

1 medium shallot, finely diced

1½ Tbsp dried breadcrumbs

2 tsp full-cream (whole) milk

40g (1½ oz) chunk of lardo or fatty pancetta, frozen

60g (2oz) Idiazabel, or other good smoked cheese, grated

4 small, soft burger buns

4 tsp Alioli (see page 246), or quality storebought

4 small leaves of butterhead or gem lettuce

4 tsp Chorizo ketchup (see page 245)

½ small red onion, very finely sliced into rings

4 pickled guindilla peppers or green chillies, to serve – optional

sea salt and black pepper

LARGE
PLATES

For all my experience in, passion for, and knowledge of the world of tapas and small plates, my absolute favourite way to share food is family-style.

Everybody sits around the table with a hunk of meat or fish as the focal point. For me, there's nothing quite like a beautifully cooked piece of meat, rested to perfection, then carried almost ceremonially to the table and finally carved... Even just writing this, I'm salivating at the thought and wishing it were Sunday. Now.

This love of the traditional family roast dinner stems from my particular food culture, which may be less exotic than the sprawling mezze spreads of the Middle East, and a far cry from the fancy restaurants that now dominate my working world, but is just as remarkable.

When I was growing up, meal times were usually rushed affairs, slotted in between other things and treated essentially as a means of sustenance, often eaten in front of the TV, perhaps on my own and sometimes with my very busy parents. But Sundays were an exception, when we'd all gather at the table. These are the times that have stayed with me, and which I now love to replicate at home with my wife and friends. There would always be a roast of some description: beef, lamb or pork (rarely chicken, come to think of it). And it would be served with a large selection of seasonal vegetables   we lived in Lincolnshire, where seasonal vegetables were the norm, even 25 years ago, and were dirt-cheap. Plus potatoes, of course: always roasted and then mashed and/or boiled, depending on who was in charge of the cooking; my dad was definitely more ambitious when it came to the spuds. Not forgetting thick gravy and all the condiments, which I still crave: mint sauce, apple sauce and peppery horseradish. Usually, my dad would carve the roast in front of us and hand out the accompaniments.

Happy memories. As a child, I loved the whole ritual, especially the sense of anticipation created by the lengthy cooking time. My slow-burning excitement was fuelled by the smells of caramelizing fat and meat that permeated every room in the house, which always had me checking on progress, getting more and more hungry as the hours slipped by. Back then, I honestly think the idealized image of sitting down as a family and breaking bread together played second fiddle to the thrill of devouring a hunk of roasted meat, but these days I'm a little more family orientated! Now, every Sunday (and occasionally on other days too), I like to labour and fuss over the roast beef, pork or lamb – or a casserole or pie, sometimes even a whole fish – before sitting down for a family-style feast with a nice bottle of wine and relishing the whole process.

So when we opened Ember Yard, how could we resist including such dishes on the menu, despite it putting a slight dent in our concept of 'small plates and tapas for sharing'? The thinking behind it was that large cuts of meat, or indeed fish, cooked for a good long time in a barbecue, and cooked well, is the stuff of dreams. Of course – brining and cold-smoking aside – it makes sense that the longer something stays in the barbecue, and the slower it cooks, the more delicious smoky flavour it's going to take on board. According to barbecue purists in the USA, cooking something for less than two hours isn't even considered barbecuing, just plain old grilling, but I won't get into the nitty-gritty of that here. For me, it all comes down to sharing – whether it's small or large plates – and the excitement that encourages.

Imagine a glorious, Florentine-style bistecca, or aged T-bone steak, cooked medium-rare, then sliced and served simply with garlic, rosemary and lemon zest; with our added twist of a little brine and smoke, and the meat reassembled around its prehistoric-looking bone, it's just such an impressive thing to bring to the table. Then there's a rich, full-flavoured hogget shoulder with North-African spices, or a leg of salt-marsh lamb with wild garlic pesto – both cooked long and slow, with the addition of a little oak wood, to intensify and naturally sweeten the flavours. When it comes to barbecued chicken, spatchcocking the bird beforehand makes for more even cooking, and brining helps to keep the meat succulent. Whole fish and shellfish hold their own on the barbecue too: try a luxurious grilled lobster for a special occasion, or a whole brill with seaweed butter for an alternative Sunday lunch.

This is where you get to show off your barbecue technique, with lots of preparation, leisurely indirect cooking and temperature checking. But then we all know that the really good stuff comes to those who wait...

The dishes in this chapter are designed to be eaten family-style, with a choice of accompaniments from the 'Sides' chapter. Compared to grazing on small plates, this may be a different way of sharing, but it's equally sociable, interactive and delicious.

Spatchcocked chicken with fig glaze, figs and sprouting broccoli

It really is worth spending a little more to buy a quality chicken. Not only is it better ethically and flavour-wise, but also a slightly older, free-range, well-fed chicken will actually cook better on the grill. Fact. This is because the water content of a battery-raised chicken will hinder the cooking and charring process as it leaches out. Here, the fruity sweetness of slowly cooked figs and fig glaze contrasts beautifully with the savoury chicken.

Pour the brine into a non-reactive container big enough to hold the chicken and pour in enough cold water to cover. Leave in the fridge for 7 hours, or overnight.

To make the fig glaze, place the fig jam or preserved figs, vinegar and 90 ml (⅓ cup) of water in a medium-sized saucepan and bring to the boil on the stovetop. Stir until the jam has melted. If you are using preserved figs, blend the glaze to a purée in a blender.

Light the barbecue and set for direct/indirect cooking. Place the lump of wood onto the ashen charcoal to start smoking.

Lift the chicken out of the brine and pat dry with paper towels. Rub over a third of the fig glaze and season with salt and pepper. Place the chicken, skin-side down, on the grill in the direct heat zone and cook for 4 minutes, to start caramelizing the skin. Turn the chicken over and transfer it to the indirect heat zone. Place a water tray in the direct heat zone and close the lid of the barbecue (the temperature inside the barbecue should be about 170°C/340°F).

After 10 minutes, baste the chicken with fig glaze and continue to cook for an hour or so, glazing it twice more during the process. When it is ready, the internal temperature of the chicken should be around 80°C (175°F), and it should be nicely glazed and caramelized. Rest the chicken in a warm spot for 20 minutes.

Meanwhile, toss the broccoli with olive oil, salt and pepper and throw onto the grill in the direct heat zone, along with the figs. Cook for about 15 minutes until the figs are soft and sticky and the broccoli nicely charred and *al dente*.

Serve the chicken on a platter with the broccoli and roast figs.

Serves 4

You'll also need a lump of hardwood, a temperature probe and a water tray

1 large (2kg/4½lb) free-range chicken, spatchcocked – ask your butcher to do this
1 quantity Brine for white meat (see page 243)
400g (14oz) sprouting broccoli, trimmed
4 large black figs, cut in half
olive oil, for cooking
sea salt and black pepper

For the fig glaze
250g (¾ cup) fig jam or preserved figs
50ml (3½ Tbsp) red wine vinegar

Slow-cooked and charcoal-grilled beef rib with horseradish sauce

If I'm going to have beef for Sunday lunch, then it's got to be rib, on the bone. It's got everything going for it: plenty of fat and beautiful meat, with more chew to it than tender cuts like fillet. What's more, the meat between the rib bones cooks to sticky-crispiness and is perfect for nibbling on. It's got to be the most impressive-looking thing too. I like to season the beef generously and then cook it really, really slowly in the oven, keeping the meat beautifully pink, before finishing it over a fierce heat on the barbecue to crisp-up and char the fat, caramelize the meat and add a barrage of smoke! This takes around 7 hours in total, so plan your day around it...

Preheat the oven to 90°C (195°F/gas mark ¼).

Remove the beef from the fridge an hour before cooking and place in a roasting tin. Rub with olive oil and season well, then sprinkle with the chopped rosemary and rub over the garlic cloves, allowing some of them to drop into the tin.

Cook the beef in the oven for about 4½ hours. Use the temperature probe to check the internal temperature: it should be around 55°C (130°F) for medium-rare, 60°C (140°F) for medium. Remove the beef from the oven and leave to rest for 40 minutes.

Light the barbecue and set for direct cooking.

Rub the beef with more olive oil and seasoning, then place on the grill, fat-side down, and let it caramelize for 5 minutes before turning and repeating on the other side. Now throw the reserved rosemary stalks and a handful of wood chips onto the coals, close the lid of the barbecue and hot-smoke the beef for 7 minutes. Open the lid and, using long-handled tongs, turn the beef onto its ends to caramelize for 2 minutes each before turning it back onto the fat side. Close the lid and cook for a further 7 minutes. When it's ready, the meat and fat should have a beautifully caramelized crust. Remove the beef from the barbecue and leave to rest for 20 minutes.

For the horseradish sauce, place the horseradish in a small bowl with the vinegar and allow to steep for 5 minutes before whisking in the crème fraiche and seasoning well.

Serve the beef on a wooden board at the table with the horseradish sauce on the side. Wood-roasted potatoes with thyme and garlic (see page 188) are a great side for this, as is Cavolo nero gratin with cream and gorgonzola (see page 168).

Serves 6–8

You'll also need a temperature probe and some oak or chestnut wood chips

1 x 3.5–4kg (7¾–9lb) beef fore-rib with 4 bones, trimmed, rolled and tied

5 sprigs rosemary, leaves picked and chopped, stalks reserved

1 garlic bulb, cloves separated and crushed

olive oil, for cooking

sea salt and black pepper

For the horseradish sauce
1 Tbsp finely grated fresh horseradish, or more to taste
1 Tbsp Cabernet Sauvignon vinegar or other red wine vinegar
250ml (generous 1 cup) crème fraiche

Marinated and roasted salt-marsh lamb leg with wild garlic pesto

I urge you to try salt-marsh lamb when it's available – generally during the latter part of spring and into early summer. The sheep graze on coastal marshland, which is abundant in herbal grasses, samphire, sorrel and sea lavenders. Such a rich and varied diet gives their meat a sweet-briny, almost floral, note. The wild garlic pesto ties in nicely with the season for salt-marsh lamb, and is a fresh, punchy counterpart to the unctuous meat. Regular new season's lamb would, of course, work brilliantly here too.

To butterfly the lamb leg, lay it skin-side down on a board and cut halfway through the centre of the leg to where the bone was. Open the meat out and cut incisions into each side of the leg to open it out further until you have a thick, even slab of meat.

Lay the lamb leg, skin-side up, in a tray or dish. Using a very sharp knife, lightly score the skin in a criss-cross fashion – this will help the marinade to penetrate. Drizzle with the olive oil, then spread over the garlic, lemon zest, anchovies, thyme, peppercorns and vinegar. Massage the marinade into the meat, then cover and transfer to the fridge. Leave for at least 3 hours, or overnight.

When ready to cook, light the barbecue and set for direct/indirect cooking. Place a lump of hardwood onto the ashen charcoal to start smoking.

Remove the lamb from the fridge 20 minutes before cooking, to let it come to room temperature. Reserve the marinade for basting later. Season the lamb with salt, then lay it skin-side down on the grill in the direct heat zone and quickly sear for 5 minutes. Turn it over and sear the other side for 5 minutes, then transfer to the indirect heat zone, still skin-side down. Close the lid of the barbecue and cook for 25 minutes (the temperature inside the barbecue should be about 170°C [340°F]). Turn over the lamb and cook for a further 20 minutes, basting with the remaining marinade a couple of times.

Meanwhile, make the wild garlic pesto. Put the parsley, garlic leaves, pine nuts and parmesan in a blender and turn on to maximum speed. Add the vinegar and then slowly pour in the olive oil. You may need to scrape down the sides and re-blend to ensure it's quite smooth. Season to taste with salt, pepper and lemon juice and set aside.

Check the internal temperature of the meat – it should be around 65°C (150°F) for pink. Remove the lamb to a plate or platter and leave to rest in a warm spot for 20 minutes. Cut the meat into chunks and serve with the pesto and any resting juices.

Serves 8 hungry people

You'll also need a lump of hardwood and a temperature probe

1 x 2.5kg (5½lb) boned leg of salt-marsh or other lamb, skin on
3 Tbsp olive oil
5 garlic cloves, finely chopped
finely grated zest of 2 lemons
40g (1½oz) salted anchovies, finely chopped
½ bunch thyme, leaves picked
1 Tbsp black peppercorns, crushed
2 Tbsp red wine vinegar
sea salt and black pepper

For the wild garlic pesto
1 small bunch flat-leaf parsley, leaves picked
handful of wild garlic (ramsons) leaves
20g (2 Tbsp) pine nuts
20g (⅓ cup) finely grated parmesan
50ml (3½ Tbsp) red wine vinegar
about 100ml (generous ⅓ cup) extra virgin olive oil
squeeze of lemon juice

Salt-baked wild bream with orange and basil

Baking fish, or indeed meat, in a salt crust is an age-old cooking method that's mainly practised in Spain and Italy. Don't be concerned about saltiness; the salt crust gently seasons the fish during the cooking, imparting a surprising sweetness. The salt cocoon also protects the fish from fierce direct heat while gently steaming it in its own self-contained 'oven'.

This is a dead-cert knockout dish for a dinner party. For maximum impact, carry the bream in its salt jacket to the table and crack open the crust, releasing the fragrant, heady aromas of the orange and basil, and revealing perfectly cooked, moist fish. Serve with Italian-style seasonal greens (see page 180) and Creamy white polenta (see page 201).

First make the salt crust by mixing the salt with a tablespoon of water to loosen. Gradually add more water – up to 3½ tablespoons altogether – until the consistency of the salt is something like wet-ish sand. You should be able to press the salt together in your hand and it will hold its shape.

Slice the orange into rounds and then cut each round in half to create semi-circles. Stuff these into the cavities of the bream, just below the head, then rip up the basil and stuff this into the cavities too. Use the cocktail sticks to skewer the cavities closed.

Take a baking tray large enough to hold the fish and spread about one third of the salt crust over the tray. Sit the bream on top, then cover the top and sides of the fish with the rest of the salt crust, leaving their tails and mouths exposed. It's very important that the main body of the fish – the part you'll be eating – is completely sealed in the salt crust to ensure it cooks properly: check it carefully, patting the crust around the fish. The fish is now ready to cook, but can be safely left in the fridge up to 4 hours before cooking.

Light the barbecue and set for direct/indirect cooking. Wait until the temperature inside the barbecue reaches 170–175°C (340–350°F; regulate with the vents, if needed), then place the tray in the indirect heat zone and close the lid. Cook for 25 minutes or until the salt crust is a pale golden brown and the internal temperature of the fish reaches 50°C (122°F) – use a temperature probe to pierce through the salt crust and check this. Remove the tray from the barbecue and leave the fish to rest for 5 minutes – it will continue to cook in the salt crust, so it's important to take it off the grill while it's still slightly under-cooked.

To serve, carry the tray to the table and, using a spoon or small knife, pull away the salt crust, starting from the head. The crust should come away easily, pulling the skin off with it; if the skin doesn't come off with the crust, just scrape it off. Once you've eaten the top half of the bream, pull out the central bone to expose the rest of the flesh. Just be careful not to eat any of the salt crust!

Serves 4–6

You'll also need 6 cocktail sticks and a temperature probe

2 large (each 1kg [2¼lb]) sea bream (or sea bass), gutted and scaled
800g (4 cups) coarse sea salt
1 small orange
½ bunch basil

Grilled lobster with smoked butter

A luxurious and majestic centrepiece to a meal, if ever there was one! Shellfish is fantastic cooked over charcoal, and the lobster shell imparts a sweet-smokiness as it becomes charred; it also helps to protect the delicate white meat against the intense heat, keeping it beautifully moist. For me, grilled lobster just has to be slathered with melted butter, and here it's smoked...

Serve this with some Crispy artichokes with lemon and sage (see page 170) or Roasted buttermilk parsnips with manchego and rosemary (see page 194).

If you have live lobsters, put them in the freezer for an hour or so (but be careful not to freeze them) – this will put them to sleep, so they can be dispatched as humanely as possible.

Light the barbecue and set for direct cooking.

On the stovetop, bring a large pan of salted water to the boil over high heat. Plunge the lobsters into the boiling water and cook for 3 minutes before removing and plunging into cold water to stop the cooking process; the lobsters will only be partly cooked at this stage.

Place the lobsters on their backs on a chopping board and, using a large, heavy-bladed knife, cut them in half lengthwise. Start by inserting the tip of the knife at base of the tail behind the head and cutting down through the tail. Next turn the lobster around and cut cleanly through the head; depending on the thickness of the shell, you may need to press the knife down to chop through it. Discard the coral and intestine from the head and crack each claw with the heel of a knife or a claw cracker. Be careful not to smash the claws completely – you just want to crack the shell and expose the meat.

Season the lobster meat and smear the tails with some of the smoked butter. Throw a good handful of wood chips on the charcoal and place the lobsters, shell-side down, on the grill. Close the lid of the barbecue and cook the lobsters for 6 minutes until the meat is just cooked through and the shell has started to blacken.

Remove the lobsters from the grill and serve with the rest of the smoked butter on the side. A lobster pick or metal skewer is handy for getting out all the small pieces of meat from the knuckles.

Serves 4

You'll also need some oak or apple chips

2 x 750g–1kg (1¾–2¼lb) lobsters, preferably native

100g (3½oz) Smoked butter (see page 244), at room temperature

sea salt and black pepper

Slow-cooked hogget shoulder with cumin, smoked paprika and buttermilk dressing

Still relatively unknown, hogget is the term for a sheep between 12 and 24 months – which makes it quite specific, neither lamb nor mutton. I've always sought out hogget, as I think you get the best of both worlds: a stronger, gamier and more intensely flavoured meat with more bite than lamb, but not as in-your-face as mutton.

This dish is a bit of a weekend project, when you have plenty of time to potter about whilst your meat is marinating, and then time for the long, slow cooking that renders it meltingly tender. It's my kind of cooking.

Lay out a large double layer of foil and place the hogget on top. Rub the meat with the olive oil, season well with salt and pepper, then rub all over with the paprika, coriander and cumin. Rub the garlic all over. Drizzle with the vinegar, then wrap up the foil to completely enclose the hogget. Leave to marinate in the fridge for at least 5 hours or overnight.

Light the barbecue and set for direct/indirect cooking. Place the water tray in the direct heat zone and put 2 lumps of wood onto the ashen charcoal to start smoking. Place the meat in the indirect heat zone and close the lid of the barbecue. (The temperature inside the barbecue should be about 180–190°C/350–375°F; regulate with the vents, if needed.) The hogget will take around 4 hours to cook. You need to turn it every hour and, after 2 hours, you'll need to top up the coals with a fresh batch from the chimney starter and add another lump of wood. Take off the foil for the last hour, to allow the meat to brown and caramelize. The hogget will become incredibly tender and melting: when it can be 'cut' with a spoon, it's ready. To be on the safe side, use the temperature probe to check the internal temperature, which should be around 75°C (167°F).

For the buttermilk dressing, simply whisk together the buttermilk, vinegar and garlic and season well.

Rest the hogget in a warm spot for 30 minutes before serving with the buttermilk dressing. I like to serve this 'pulled' into shreds using two forks and then wrapped in Potato and honey flatbreads (see page 56) with a crisp green salad and finely sliced red onions.

Serves 4–6

You'll also need 3 lumps of oak wood, a chimney starter, a water tray and a temperature probe

1 x 2.5–3kg (5½–6¾lb) whole hogget or lamb shoulder, bone in
50ml (3½ Tbsp) olive oil
3 Tbsp smoked paprika
4 Tbsp crushed coriander seeds
2 Tbsp ground cumin
8 garlic cloves, roughly chopped
50ml (3½ Tbsp) red wine vinegar
sea salt and black pepper

For the buttermilk dressing
100ml (generous ⅓ cup) buttermilk
20ml (1½ Tbsp) white wine vinegar
2 garlic cloves, finely chopped

Florentine-style steak

This is inspired by both the *bistecca Fiorentina* found the length and breadth of Florence and across the rest of Tuscany, and by a love of brilliant beef. The classic Fiorentina is a T-bone cut from local beasts, usually the Chianina breed, and then grilled very rare, sliced and served with chopped raw garlic, rosemary and maybe some lemon. The dish has acquired something of a cult status in Italy, where there are several staunch schools of thought on its preparation and execution. This passionate debate is typical of the Italians' approach to food and its wider cultural context, and I love them for it.

I've added a quick brining, followed by some cold-smoking to give it a super-smoky boost. After this, you'll need to rest the meat for a few hours – but, boy, is it worth it!

Submerge the steaks in the brine in a non-reactive container and leave for 1 hour.

Light and set the cold-smoking device in the barbecue. Place the steaks on the rack in the barbecue and smoke for 2 hours and 20 minutes. Transfer the steaks to a bowl, then cover and allow to rest in the fridge for at least 4 hours, or overnight.

Light the barbecue and set for direct/indirect cooking.

Season the steaks, rub with a little olive oil and then place on the grill over the direct heat zone. Cook for 3 minutes until nicely charred and caramelized, then turn over and cook for a further 3 minutes before moving to the perimeter of the indirect heat zone for 2 minutes to rest. These cooking times will give you medium-rare steaks – if you want them cooked further, i.e. medium, then add another 2 minutes on each side to the cooking time.

Transfer the steaks to a chopping board. Cut the meat off the bone, then thickly slice each piece before reassembling. Transfer to a clean board or platter, drizzle with extra virgin olive oil and sprinkle over the garlic, rosemary and lemon zest.

This is great with Wood-roasted potatoes with thyme and garlic (see page 188), which you can cook just before the steak goes on and keep warm for a few minutes – all seriously delicious.

Serves 4

You'll need a cold-smoking device and some oak wood dust for this recipe

2 x 1kg (2¼lb) T-bone steaks or 2 x 600g (1¼lb) sirloin or rump steaks of similar thickness

1 quantity Brine for red meat (see page 243)

3 garlic cloves, finely chopped

2 sprigs rosemary, leaves finely chopped

finely grated zest of 1 lemon

olive oil, for cooking

extra virgin olive oil, for drizzling

sea salt and black pepper

Barbecued brill with seaweed butter

Brill is the unsung hero of the flat-fish world. Not as glamorous (or as expensive) as its cousin the turbot, it is equally sweet and delicious, with firm, meaty flesh. I first tried whole brill cooked over charcoal at a restaurant in San Sebastian in Spain. It was fantastic, and I loved it so much that I came home with a specially designed fish-grilling basket. You can pick these up at kitchenware stores and online, but alternatively some careful spatula action will work fine.

The seaweed butter is an unusual but relevant intriguing addition to the brill. Sea lettuce is the preferred seaweed for this, although you could also use samphire or sea purslane; your fishmonger should be happy to help.

Light the barbecue and set for direct cooking.

Roughly chop the seaweed, then mix it through the butter. Season well with salt and pepper and set aside.

Season the brill on both sides and clamp into the fish-grilling basket, if you have one. Put the fish on the grill and cook for 6 minutes on each side until the skin is charred and the flesh is opaque – check this just below the head, where the fish is at its fattest.

Generously dot the butter onto the fish and let it melt over the flesh before squeezing over the lemon juice and transferring to a serving board or platter.

Serves 4

You'll also need a fish-grilling basket, if possible, or just a large spatula

70g (2½oz) seaweed, any dry stalks removed if using purslane

125g (½ cup) unsalted butter, at room temperature

1 x 1.6kg (3½lb) whole brill, guts and fins removed

juice of ½ lemon

sea salt and black pepper

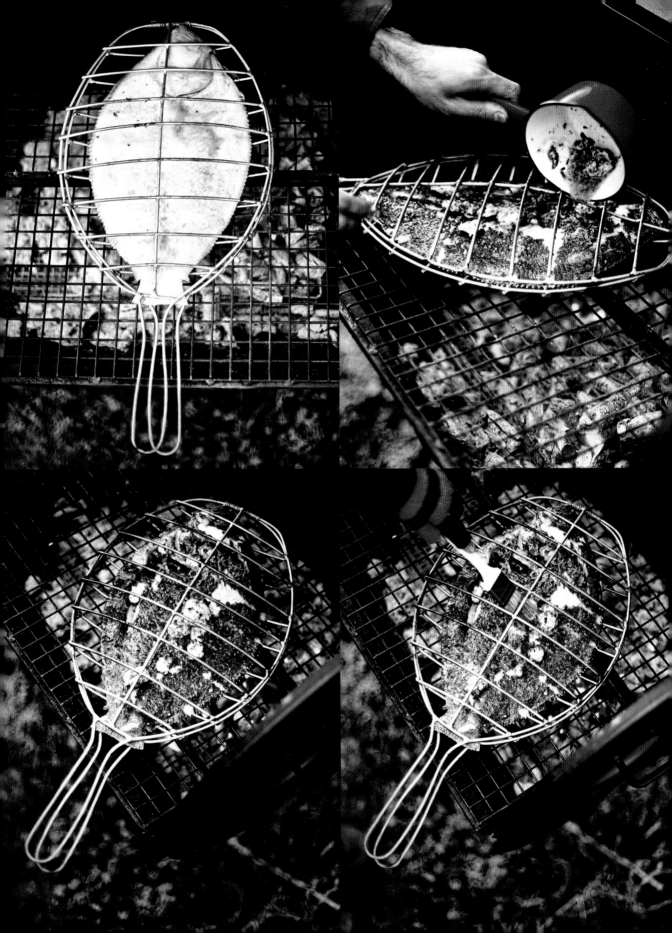

Honey-basted duck with fondant fennel

Is it me, or has a whole roast duck become little more than a distant memory from the 80s? Chinese restaurants excluded, you rarely see them now – it always seems to be breasts and legs cooked separately – but, for me, there's nothing like a glistening, mahogany-lacquered bird with crispy skin and succulent meat. I think it's the fattiness that scares some people; however, if you render the fat properly there won't be an excessive amount, and it will be balanced by the meat and skin. The aniseed note of the fennel helps to cut the richness, and is a match made in heaven.

Place the duck in a non-reactive container and pour over the brine. Cover and leave to cure in the fridge for 5 hours.

Lift the duck out of the brine and pat dry with paper towels. Using a roasting fork or a skewer, prick the skin of the duck all over – this will help to release the fat from under the skin during cooking, resulting in crispier skin.

Light the barbecue and set for direct/indirect cooking. Place the lumps of wood onto the ashen coals to start smoking.

Trim the ends from the fennel, then cut each bulb lengthwise into quarters. Place the fennel in the roasting pan and sit the duck on top. Season with salt and pepper, then pour about 250ml (1 cup) of water around the fennel and add the star anise and bay leaves. The water will help to cook the fennel and steam the underside of the duck, keeping the meat moist and creating a delicious gravy. Very useful!

Place the pan in the direct heat zone and close the lid of the barbecue (the temperature inside the barbecue should be about 220–230°C/425–450°F). Cook the duck for 20 minutes, then brush with honey and cook for a further 20 minutes, still with the lid down. Transfer the pan to the indirect heat zone and cook for 20 more minutes, topping up the water as necessary to keep about 200ml (¾ cup) in the base of the pan.

When it's ready, the duck should have a crisp, mahogany skin, the fennel should be very tender and glazed, and the fatty juices in the pan should have started to reduce. To be on the safe side, use the temperature probe to check the internal temperature of the duck, which should be around 60°C (140°F). At this temperature, the duck meat will still be pink; for well done, cook the duck for another 20 minutes.

Remove from the barbecue and leave to rest in a warm spot for 20 minutes. Place the duck on a chopping board, transfer the fennel to a serving dish and keep both warm. Strain the cooking juices through a fine sieve into a small saucepan and place over medium heat on the stovetop. Carefully skim off the fat with a ladle and, if necessary, simmer the juices for a couple minutes to reduce to a gravy consistency.

Serve the duck and fennel with a jug of gravy alongside.

Serves 4–6

You'll also need a temperature probe, 2 lumps of hardwood and a roasting pan large enough to hold the duck and fit in your barbecue!

1 x 2.5kg (5½lb) oven-ready duck

3 quantities Brine for red meat (see page 243)

2 medium fennel bulbs

2 star anise

2 bay leaves

100ml (6½ Tbsp) runny honey

sea salt and black pepper

Roasted and grilled pork ribs with quince glaze

Writing a barbecue book, I just had to include some ribs. These have been on the menu at Ember Yard since we opened, and will probably never come off. We use Ibérico pork and if you can source this online or at a specialist butcher, then I highly recommend it. Membrillo (quince cheese, paste or jelly) is a classic Spanish condiment to accompany cheese. It is made by cooking quinces, long and slow, to a puree, then set with natural pectin from the fruit. It's available at Spanish food suppliers or good supermarkets. Melting it down to a thick syrup and adding vinegar for acidity makes a brilliant rib glaze, and it's easy too!

Preheat the oven to 180°C (350°F/gas mark 4).

Place the rib racks in a large roasting tin and pour in 3 litres (3 quarts) of water, then add the salt, peppercorns and bay leaves. Cover the tin with foil, transfer to the oven and cook for about 1½ hours, or until the ribs are very soft and tender – you should be able to pull out a bone quite easily. Remove the ribs from the tin and leave to cool for an hour or so to firm up.

Meanwhile, make the quince glaze. Place all the ingredients in a medium saucepan with 300ml (1¼ cups) of water and stir over low heat on the stovetop until the quince paste has completely melted.

Light the barbecue and set for direct/indirect cooking. Place the lump of wood onto the ashen charcoal to start smoking.

Brush the ribs with the glaze, then place on the grill in the direct heat zone. Cook for 2 minutes on each side before moving them to the indirect heat zone and basting with the glaze. Close the lid of the barbecue and continue to cook the ribs, turning and basting them every 3 minutes or so, until they are beautifully glazed and lightly charred with a good crust.

I like to serve these ribs with extra warm glaze on the side for dipping, and perhaps a Seasonal salad of heritage carrots (see page 192) and Patatas aliñadas (see page 174).

Serves 4

You'll also need a lump of oak or beech hardwood

1 x 1.2kg (2¾lb) rack of Ibérico or Gloucester Old Spot pork ribs
1½ Tbsp coarse sea salt
10 black peppercorns
3 bay leaves

For the quince glaze
200g (7oz) quince paste (membrillo)
50ml (3½ Tbsp) white balsamic vinegar
50g (¼ cup) dark brown sugar

Hot-smoked pork belly with cider, apples and marjoram

The classic combination of pork, apple and cider has been around for years. It is said that this culinary triumvirate first came into being in Normandy, where all three elements are in plentiful supply. When I was young, my parents would cook pork chops with grilled apples and cider gravy, and I remember thinking how exotic and interesting the dish was (I think it's still rolled out in the Tish senior household on special occasions). You'll need to start this recipe the day before.

There's only one non-negotiable in this book... and that's serving this pork with Smoked mashed potato (see page 200).

Using a very sharp knife, score the skin of the pork belly in criss-cross fashion. Place the pork in a non-reactive bowl or container, then pour over the brine and 3 litres (3 quarts) of water. Leave for 7–8 hours in the fridge.

For the cider glaze, place the sugar and vinegar in a non-reactive saucepan and heat on the stovetop until the sugar has dissolved. Pour in the cider. Bring to the boil, then reduce to a simmer and cook until thick and syrupy. Reserve and keep warm.

Light the barbecue and set for direct/indirect cooking. Place the lump of wood onto the ashen charcoal to start smoking.

Lift the pork out of the brine and pat dry with paper towels. Rub the meat all over with some of the glaze, then place skin-side down on the grill in the direct heat zone. Cook for 3 minutes before turning and cooking for 3 minutes on the other side. Transfer the pork, skin-side down, to the indirect heat zone. Place a water tray in the direct heat zone. Baste the pork with the glaze, then close the lid (the temperature inside the barbecue should be about 170–175°C/340–350°F; regulate with the vents, if needed) and cook for 1 hour before turning and basting the pork again. Cook for another hour, then turn and baste again.

At this stage, check if the water tray needs topping up, and add a fresh batch of coals from the chimney starter and another lump of wood. Place the apples on the grill around the pork and cook with the lid closed for a further hour, then baste the pork again. Check to see if the pork is very tender – it should be soft enough to cut with a spoon. If not, keep cooking and basting for another hour or so. To be on the safe side, use the temperature probe to check the internal temperature of the pork, which should be around 75°C (167°F).

Finish with a final glaze, then remove the pork from the barbecue and leave in a warm spot to rest for 20 minutes. The apples can come out at the same time as the pork, as long as they are nice and soft.

Cut the pork into into four thick slices, and serve each one with an apple and a sprinkle of marjoram leaves.

Serves 4

You'll also need a lump of hardwood, a chimney starter, a water tray and a temperature probe

1.2 kg (2¾lb) boneless pork belly, skin on

1 quantity Brine for white meat (see page 243)

4 small apples

½ bunch marjoram, leaves picked, to serve

sea salt and black pepper

For the cider glaze

100g (½ cup) dark brown sugar

50ml (3½ Tbsp) cider vinegar

500ml (generous 2 cups) dry cider

Grilled crab with fennel, lemon and alioli

You can buy pots of white and brown crabmeat in supermarkets, and they are certainly convenient. However, pristine meat picked straight from a fresh crab is a revelation. Sure, it's quite messy, but there's much fun to be had breaking and cracking the shells, then getting stuck into the sweet flesh. This is a dish of two halves: the legs and claws grilled; then the brown crabmeat (my favourite), mixed with raw fennel and grilled in the shell. Serve with plenty of flatbreads to mop up the juices. Absolutely delicious!

Your fishmonger should be able to source live coastal crabs, such as brown and Dungeness. If a live crab is a bit too much, frozen crabs make a good substitute.

If you have live crabs, put them in the freezer for an hour – this will put them to sleep, so they can be dispatched as humanely as possible.

On the stovetop, bring a large pan of salted water to the boil over high heat. Plunge the crabs into the boiling water and cook for 3 minutes before removing and plunging into cold water to stop the cooking process; the crabs will only be partly cooked at this stage.

Drain the crabs, then place them on their backs on a chopping board. Remove the triangular flap from their base and then insert your thumb or a rounded knife into this same spot and prise off the top of the crab shell (carapace). Remove the feathery gills and any intestine – you just want to keep the creamy brown crabmeat. Break off the claws and legs and discard the central body. Crack each claw and leg with the heel of a knife or a claw cracker and each of the legs. Be careful not to smash them completely – you just want to crack the shell and expose the meat. Now you are ready to grill.

Light the barbecue and set for direct cooking.

Pour the olive oil into a small saucepan and add the fennel seeds, garlic and the zest and juice of one of the lemons. Heat the pan on the barbecue until the oil starts to bubble, then cook for 2 minutes before pouring into a bowl.

Brush the shells of the crab legs, claws and the inside of the carapace with the fennel oil. Stuff the sliced raw fennel into the carapace, along with the brown crabmeat, some seasoning and another good drizzle of the fennel oil.

Place all the crab parts on the grill and cook the legs for 2 minutes each side, and the claws for 3 minutes each side. Cook the carapace (without turning it!) for 5 minutes or until bubbling and the brown crabmeat is thickened and creamy.

Serve all the crab bits together on a platter, along with the alioli, the remaining fennel oil and lemon quarters.

Serves 4

2 x 1.5kg (3¼ lb) brown or Dungeness crabs

100ml (generous ⅓ cup) extra virgin olive oil

2 tsp fennel seeds

1 garlic clove, finely sliced

2 unwaxed lemons

1 small fennel bulb, finely sliced

sea salt and black pepper

1 quantity Alioli (see page 246), to serve

Pork shoulder cooked in milk with bay and cinnamon

This old-fashioned and unusual Italian method of cooking meat is a real joy. As the meat slowly cooks, the aromatic milk boils down, mixing with the porky juices and creating delicious rich curds and its own sauce. Cooking this way requires some time, but once you've got it going you can just sit back and wait, in anticipation of a good feed. Creamy white polenta with fennel seeds and chilli (see page 201) is my favourite accompaniment here.

Pour the brine over the pork in a non-reactive container, then cover and leave to cure in the fridge for 3 hours.

Light the barbecue and set for direct/indirect cooking. Place 2 lumps of wood onto the coals to start smoking.

Remove the pork from the brine and dry with paper towels. Place the pork, skin-side up, in the ovenproof pot and pour in some of the milk – leave the top of the pork protruding, so it will caramelize during the cooking. Drop the bay leaves and cinnamon sticks into the milk around the pork, then place the pot in the direct heat zone and bring the milk to the boil.

Move the pot to the indirect heat zone and close the lid of the barbecue (the temperature inside the barbecue should be about 170°C/340°F; regulate with the vents, if needed). Cook for 2 hours, then check on it: the milk should be bubbling away and separating into curds, and the pork skin should have taken on a golden hue. Top up the pot with some more milk, still leaving the top of the pork uncovered. At this stage, you'll also need to top up the coals with a fresh batch from the chimney starter and add another lump of wood. Close the lid again and cook for a further 1½ hours.

When it's done, the pork meat should be soft and tender, and the skin browned and crisp. To be on the safe side, use the temperature probe to check the internal temperature, which should be around 75°C (167°F). If the pork needs longer, top up the milk again and keep cooking until it's ready.

Remove from the barbecue and leave to rest for 30 minutes. Using a ladle, skim off the fat from the milky-curd sauce and transfer the meat to a serving platter. Taste the sauce and season, if necessary, then whisk to break up the curds (the sauce will look separated, but this is as it should be).

<u>Serves 4–6</u>

You'll also need 3 lumps of hardwood, a chimney starter and a good, sturdy ovenproof pot or casserole large enough to hold the big lump of pork

1 x 3kg (6½lb) pork shoulder, bone in and skin on

2 quantities Brine for white meat (see page 243)

about 4L (4qt) full-cream (whole) milk

8 bay leaves

2 cinnamon sticks

Grilled free-range chicken with yogurt, lemon and North-African spices

Over the past couple of years I've really got into the flavours of North Africa and the Levant – something to do with being challenged by the different, unusual and exciting spices, I suspect. They are also delicious, and I love spending time travelling in and experiencing this part of the world.

Spatchcocking a chicken is by far the best way to go when cooking it on a barbecue – it's quicker and the chicken cooks much more evenly. Your butcher should be able to this for you. Start this recipe a day ahead.

Pour the brine into a non-reactive container big enough to hold the chicken. Immerse the chicken in the brine and pour in enough cold water to cover. Leave in the fridge for 7 hours, or overnight.

Remove the chicken from the brine, pat dry with paper towels and place in a bowl or on a tray. Using a pestle and mortar, roughly crush all the spices (if you don't have a pestle and mortar, improvise with a small bowl and the end of a rolling pin), then mix with the yogurt. Squeeze the juice of one of the lemons over the chicken, then smother it with the yogurt-spice mix and the olive oil. Cover and leave to marinate in the fridge for at least 2 hours.

Set and light a barbecue for direct/indirect cooking. Place the lump of wood onto the ashen charcoal to start smoking.

Season the chicken with salt and pepper and place it, skin-side down, on the grill in the direct heat zone. Cook for 5 minutes to char the skin, then turn it over a cook for a further 5 minutes before moving it to the indirect heat zone. Position the water tray in the direct heat zone and close the lid of the barbecue. Cook the chicken for about 1 hour (the temperature inside the barbecue should be about 170–175°C/340–350°F; regulate with the vents, if needed). To be on the safe side, use the temperature probe to check the internal temperature of the chicken, which should be around 75°C (167°F). Remove the chicken from the grill and leave to rest in a warm spot for 20 minutes.

Meanwhile, cut the remaining lemons in half and place them, cut-side down, in the direct heat zone. Cook for 20 minutes until soft and caramelized.

Pour the resting juices from the chicken into the extra seasoned yogurt and stir through. Serve the chicken with the yogurt and the caramelized lemon halves for squeezing over.

Serves 4

You'll also need a lump of hardwood, a water tray and a temperature probe

1 large (2kg [4½lb]) free-range chicken, spatchcocked
1 quantity Brine for white meat (see page 243)
1½ Tbsp fennel seeds
1 Tbsp coriander seeds
2 tsp cumin seeds
2 Tbsp smoked paprika
2 Tbsp sumac
1½ Tbsp ground cumin
1 Tbsp dried chilli flakes
100g (½ cup) Greek yogurt
3 unwaxed lemons
75ml (scant ⅓ cup) extra virgin olive oil
sea salt and black pepper
extra yogurt, seasoned with salt, pepper and sumac, to serve

Paella

Done well, this is really the perfect party dish – and cooking paella on the barbecue adds that extra touch of smoke and flame to proceedings. It's highly visual, exciting, mouthwateringly delicious, and everyone can serve themselves with as much or as little as they like. I'm a big fan of meat and fish combinations – and the paella traditionalists I've spoken to would argue it's not paella unless there's a mix – but feel free to make this your own by increasing the quantities of whichever seafood or meat you like and leaving out the rest. A proper paella pan makes all the difference, of course, and the good news is they're cheap and widely available.

Light the barbecue and set for direct cooking.

Set your paella pan in the direct heat zone of the barbecue and add a lug of olive oil. Throw in the chorizo and cook for 2 minutes, stirring briskly, to release its paprika-infused juices. Add the chicken or rabbit and brown on each side before adding the onion, garlic, peppers and chilli. Cook for 5–6 minutes, stirring as you go, until everything has softened but not coloured. Now add the paprika, rice and saffron and stir everything together well. Season with salt and pepper, then stir in the wine, sherry, stock and tomatoes and leave to cook for 12 minutes without stirring. The idea with paella is that you let the rice in contact with the base and sides of the pan lightly caramelize – unlike a risotto.

Now stir the mussels into the rice and place the squid and prawns on top of the rice, without stirring them through. If the rice is looking too dry, add a little water at this stage. Throw a handful of wood chips onto the coals, then close the lid of the barbecue and cook the paella for 8 minutes, by which time the rice and seafood should be just cooked through. Squeeze over some lemon juice, sprinkle over the parsley and serve.

Serves about 6

You'll also need a paella pan or large ovenproof frying pan and some oak, apple or birch wood chips

- 250g (9oz) spicy cooking chorizo, skin removed, roughly chopped
- 2 large chicken thighs or rabbit legs, boned, cut into bite-size pieces
- 1 large onion, finely chopped
- 2 garlic cloves, finely chopped
- 2 small red (bell) peppers, deseeded and finely chopped
- 1 chilli, finely chopped
- 1 Tbsp smoked paprika
- 500g (18oz) paella [ie Bomba] or Calasparra short-grain rice
- 1 tsp saffron threads, infused in 1 tsp warm water
- 200ml (generous ¾ cup) dry white wine
- 200ml (generous ¾ cup) dry sherry, such as fino
- 200ml (generous ¾ cup) good fish or chicken stock, ideally homemade
- 500g (18oz) plum tomatoes, finely chopped (with skin and seeds)
- 200g (7oz) mussels, cleaned and debearded
- 200g (7oz) squid, cleaned and cut into bite-size pieces
- 6 large tiger prawns (shrimp), shell on
- juice of 1 lemon
- ½ bunch flat-leaf parsley, finely chopped, stalks and all
- olive oil, for cooking
- sea salt and black pepper

Barbecued pheasant in lardo with porcini, crispy garlic and truffle butter

This is like autumn on a plate: pheasant, one of the finest and most eagerly anticipated of the game birds, served with mushrooms and some decadent black truffle, all evocative of the season's earthy charms.

Game is generally very lean, since it is constantly on the move and truly wild. With this in mind, it's important to take care when cooking it to prevent the meat drying out. Here, the pheasant is brined and then wrapped in lardo (cured pork back fat) to baste and lubricate the meat during its time on the grill.

Submerge the pheasants in the brine in a non-reactive container and leave in the fridge for 2½ hours.

Light the barbecue and set for direct/indirect cooking. Place the lump of wood on the ashen coals to start smoking.

Make the truffle butter by mixing all the ingredients together and seasoning to taste.

Lift the pheasants out of the brine and pat dry with paper towels. Drizzle the pheasants with olive oil and season all over with salt and pepper.

Lay the strips of lardo out on a tray so they overlap and form two rectangles large enough to wrap around the birds. Spoon about a teaspoon of truffle butter onto the breast of each pheasant, then lay breast-side down in the middle of the lardo rectangle. Fold over the ends of the strips of lardo to seal, pressing carefully to 'mould' the fat to the birds, then transfer to the fridge and leave to firm up for 20 minutes.

Place the pheasants, breast-side up, on the grill in the indirect heat zone and close the lid (the temperature inside the barbecue should be about 170°C/ 340°F). Leave to cook for 25 minutes, then transfer to the direct heat zone, breast-side down, and cook each breast for 2–3 minutes to caramelize. Check the internal temperature: a temperature probe inserted into the leg should read about 60°C (140°F). Remove the pheasants from the barbecue, slather with plenty of truffle butter (but save some to cook the mushrooms!) and leave to rest in a warm spot for 10 minutes.

Place a heavy-based frying pan on the grill in the direct heat zone and add the remaining truffle butter. When it's foaming, add the mushrooms and season well. Cook the mushrooms until tender and starting to caramelize, then add the garlic slices and continue to cook until the mushrooms and garlic are golden brown. Immediately remove from the heat and transfer the mushrooms and garlic to a serving platter. Pour the cooking juices from the pan over the pheasants.

Serve the pheasants whole on the platter with the mushrooms and garlic. Pour the buttery resting juices into a jug and serve on the side.

Serves 4

You'll also need a lump of hardwood and a temperature probe

1 quantity Brine for red meat (see page 243)

2 oven-ready pheasants

50g (2oz) lardo or pancetta, finely sliced into strips

200g (7oz) porcini mushrooms, or other large meaty mushrooms, such as king oyster, cleaned and thickly sliced

2 garlic cloves, very finely sliced

olive oil, for cooking

sea salt and black pepper

For the truffle butter

100g (½ cup) unsalted butter, softened to room temperature

1 Tbsp white truffle oil

3g (⅛ oz) black truffle, finely chopped – optional, but delicious!

SIDES

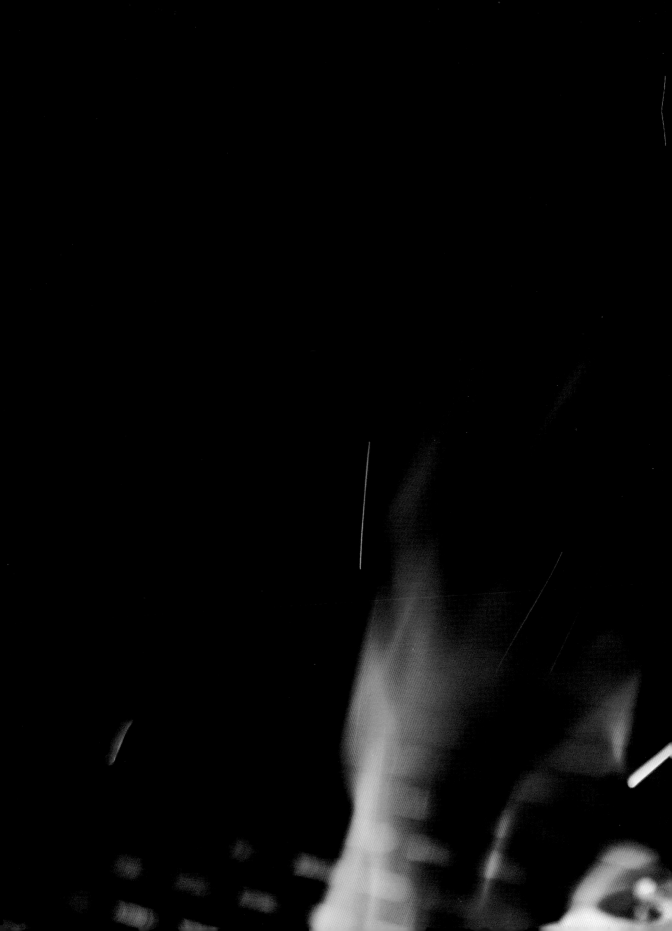

Having just cooked, tested
and eaten all the recipes here,
I think many could almost be
stand-alone dishes.

However, the original idea behind this chapter was – and still is,
for the most part – that it would be great to serve one or more of
these alongside the larger plates to share, in effect making a lovely
family-style sharing meal that you might have for Sunday lunch
or, if you're lucky, a few times a week.

Anyway, these dishes are very simple to prepare, and as most of
them require some kind of barbecue action – whether grilling,
smoking or cooking over charcoal to infuse them with flavour
– it makes sense to factor them into a bigger meal, so you're not
lighting your barbecue just to cook some potatoes. Other dishes
are simply cooked on the stovetop in your kitchen, but will still
complement whatever else you're cooking on the barbecue. And
if you want to incorporate some of these dishes into a small-plate
tapas or mezze spread, then I think that would be fantastic too.

My recommendations are purely to get you started; it all comes
down to what you want to do and experimenting to see what
works. Oh, but there's one absolute must-have combination that
really shouldn't be messed around with, in my humble opinion,
and that's serving Smoked mashed potato (see page 200) with
Hot-smoked pork belly with cider, apple and marjoram (see page
148) – that one's written in stone!

Cavolo nero gratin with cream and gorgonzola

An indulgent side, if ever there was one, but so delicious. You can use any other seasonal cabbage for this, such as savoy, hispi or even Brussels sprouts. The chunky breadcrumbs add a great crunch. I like to cook and serve this in an ovenproof, terracotta pie dish. Serve with lamb, beef or pork.

Trim any tough stalks from the cabbage and tear the leaves from the stems. Cook the leaves in boiling salted water on the stovetop for 3 minutes until just cooked and then rinse under the cold tap to refresh. Drain the leaves, squeezing out all the excess water, then chop roughly and reserve.

Pour the cream into a small saucepan and add the garlic. Place over medium heat on the stovetop and reduce by half – watch it carefully, as cream has a tendency to boil over!

Transfer the cabbage to a pie or gratin dish and season well. Dot the gorgonzola in lumps among the cabbage, then pour over the reduced cream (including the sliced garlic). Place in the fridge to chill for at least 1 hour.

Light the barbecue and set for indirect cooking.

Pulse the bread to coarse, irregular crumbs in a food processor, then toss with a little olive oil, salt and pepper. Sprinkle over the top of the cabbage, then put the dish in the middle of the indirect heat zone of the barbecue and close the lid. Cook the gratin for 20 minutes, or until the cream is bubbling and the breadcrumbs are golden brown.

Serves 4

500g (18oz) cavolo nero, or other cabbage

250ml (generous 1 cup) double (heavy) cream

2 garlic cloves, thinly sliced

100g (3½oz) gorgonzola, or other creamy blue cheese

2 slices of day-old bread, crust removed

olive oil, for cooking

sea salt and black pepper

Olive-oil mash with slow-cooked garlic

I've been making olive-oil-whipped mash for many years, so I thought I'd develop it with the addition of some slow-cooked, caramel-y garlic. If you get a taste for this, throw some garlic bulbs on the barbecue when you're doing other stuff and have them ready to use in the fridge, where they'll keep for at least a week.

Light the barbecue and set for indirect cooking.

Wrap the garlic in foil and use long-handled tongs to nestle it in the coals. The garlic will take about 1 hour to become soft and tender. Remove and leave to cool slightly before unwrapping the foil, cutting the very top off the bulb and then squeezing the soft cloves of garlic out onto a chopping board. Chop to form a rough paste.

Evenly dice the potatoes and cook slowly in a pan of simmering salted water on the stovetop, until nice and tender. Drain then return to the hot pan and let the potatoes steam-dry for a few minutes before pressing through a potato ricer or masher.

Heat the cream in a small saucepan over medium heat to reduce by about a third before stirring into the mash, along with the butter. Finally, whisk in the olive oil and stir in the garlic paste. I really like garlic, so I add the lot, but you may like a little less. Season the mash and serve immediately.

Serves 4

1 large garlic bulb

1kg (2¼lb) Desiree potatoes, peeled

100ml (generous ⅓ cup) double (heavy) cream

50g (3½ Tbsp) diced unsalted butter, at room temperature

2 Tbsp good-quality extra virgin olive oil

sea salt and black pepper

Crispy artichokes with lemon and sage

You can use either baby globe artichokes or larger ones for this recipe. To be honest, this could just as easily have made its appearance in the 'Tapas and small plates' chapter, as these artichokes are delicious on their own or as a salty snack with an aperitif. I love serving them with grilled fish as a take on good old fish and chips. Cook these either on your barbecue or on the stovetop.

If cooking on the barbecue, light and set for direct/indirect cooking.

Drain the cooked artichokes and leave to cool, then slice them very thinly lengthwise using a sharp knife. Dust with flour, ensuring the artichoke slices are completely coated.

Heat a 3cm (1¼in) depth of olive oil in a medium saucepan until very hot, either in the direct heat zone of your barbecue or on the stovetop. Check the oil is hot enough by carefully, with a pair of tongs, dipping the corner of an artichoke slice into the oil: if it sizzles straightaway, the oil is ready.

Quickly fry the sage leaves in the hot oil until crisp. Scoop them out with a slotted spoon and drain well on paper towels.

Working in batches, gently slip the artichoke slices into the oil and cook until crisp and golden brown. Using a slotted spoon, remove from the oil and drain on paper towels.

Season the artichokes with salt and pepper, then scatter over the crispy sage leaves and serve with lemon wedges on the side.

<u>Serves 4</u>

8 baby globe artichokes or 4 regular ones, prepared and cooked (see page 82)
plain (all-purpose) flour, for dusting
olive oil, for deep-frying
16–20 sage leaves
1 lemon, cut into wedges
sea salt and black pepper

Slow-cooked autumn roots with maple syrup

Really you can use any root vegetables you have around for this but I'd avoid red beetroot, simply because they have a tendency to stain anything they're cooked with. Try to select roots of roughly the same size, or cut them down accordingly. These are perfect with a big roast, such as chicken or beef – just pop them on an hour or so before the roast will be ready. Alternatively, they can be cooked in advance and reheated.

Light the barbecue and set for direct/indirect cooking.

Wash and peel the vegetables, then cut up as needed to make them all roughly the same size. Place the vegetables in a roasting tin, along with the garlic, thyme and rosemary. Dot the butter over the vegetables and season with salt and pepper.

Cover with foil, place in the indirect heat zone and close the lid of the barbecue. Cook for about 1 hour, then open the lid and check the vegetables – they should be tender and have started to caramelize and turn golden. If they are softening but not browning, remove the foil and transfer to the direct heat zone for a few minutes to speed up the process.

Drizzle over the maple syrup and stir the vegetables to coat before serving.

Serves 4–6

1.2kg (2¾lb) mixed root vegetables, such as carrots, swede (rutabaga), turnips, celeriac, parsnip
1 garlic bulb, cut in half
4 sprigs thyme
1 sprig rosemary
50g (3½ Tbsp) unsalted butter, diced
1 Tbsp maple syrup
sea salt and black pepper

Patatas aliñadas with piquillo peppers and wild garlic

I've given this classic Spanish potato dish a twist by cooking the potatoes over charcoal first (as opposed to boiling them), before crushing them with smoked hot paprika and two different peppers: raw green for freshness, and piquillo for smoky-sweetness. Wild garlic leaves are in season for only a few weeks of the year, at the start of spring. They're delicious and fresh-tasting, adding a different type of garlicky kick, but don't worry if they're not around – you can use some young new season's or 'wet' garlic instead.

Light the barbecue and set for direct/indirect cooking.

Place the potatoes on the grill in the centre of the indirect cooking zone and close the lid of the barbecue. Cook the potatoes for 45 minutes or until the skins have crisped and lightly charred and the flesh is soft and tender. Transfer the potatoes to a bowl, cover with cling film and leave to steam for 10 minutes.

Roughly crush the potatoes, still with their skins on, with the back of a fork, then add both kinds of peppers, along with the garlic, paprika, oil and vinegar. Mix well, crushing the potatoes a little more with the fork to ensure their flesh is exposed to all the flavours. Season well, then cover and leave to marinate at room temperature for an hour before serving.

Serves 4

600g (21oz) Charlotte, Pink Fir Apple or other waxy potatoes, cleaned but skins on

80g (3oz) piquillo peppers, roughly chopped

1 small green (bell) pepper, deseeded and finely chopped

small handful of wild garlic (ramsons) leaves, chopped, or 3 'wet' garlic cloves, finely sliced

2 tsp smoked hot paprika

2 Tbsp extra virgin olive oil

2 Tbsp red wine vinegar

sea salt and black pepper

Smoked peppers, shallots and tomatoes with oregano

This is simply a selection of grilled peppers, firm-fleshed tomatoes and sweet shallots that's perfect with my Florentine-style steak (see page 134). Use plenty of oak wood chips if you want to create a super-smokiness. I tend to make a good amount of this and store it in jars in the fridge, as the flavour only improves over time – just transfer the marinated vegetables to Kilner-style jars, then seal and keep in the fridge for up to 4 weeks.

Light the barbecue and set for direct/indirect cooking. If you want to boost the wood-smoke flavour, sprinkle a handful of oak chips over the charcoal.

Place the whole peppers on the grill in the indirect heat zone, along with the shallots, skin-side down. Place the tomatoes, skin-side down, in the direct heat zone. Close the lid of the barbecue and cook for 5 minutes before turning all the vegetables over and adding another handful of wood chips. Close the lid and cook for 5–6 minutes or until the peppers and shallots have started to soften and the tomatoes have caramelized. Remove the tomatoes from the grill and set aside. Continue to cook the peppers and shallots until they are soft.

Transfer the peppers to a bowl, cover with cling film and leave to steam for 10 minutes. Peel off the skins and discard the seeds, then slice the peppers into rough strips. Peel the shallots and cut each one into 3 or 4 pieces. Place the peppers, shallots and tomatoes in a bowl and add the olive oil, vinegar and oregano. Stir gently to coat the vegetables in the oil and vinegar, then leave to marinate in the fridge for at least 4 hours.

Bring to room temperature before serving.

Serves 4–6

You'll also need some oak chips, if you want an extra-smoky flavour

3 medium red (bell) peppers
3 medium yellow (bell) peppers
3 banana shallots, cut in half, skin intact
3 plum tomatoes, cut in half
3 Tbsp extra virgin olive oil
2 Tbsp balsamic vinegar
2 tsp oregano leaves

Barbecued mushrooms with rosemary, garlic and soy butter

My favourite mushrooms for cooking on the barbecue are the meaty ones: porcini, king oyster or big flat portobellos. You need firm, sturdy fungi to stand up to the heat of the charcoal and develop a crust while staying juicy inside – rather like a good piece of meat. These would be heavenly with the Slow-cooked and charcoal-grilled beef rib (see page 123).

Light the barbecue and set for direct/indirect cooking.

Place the butter in a bowl and stir through the garlic, chopped rosemary leaves and soy sauce, then season with pepper. Reserve at room temperature.

Wipe the mushrooms with damp paper towels to clean, if necessary, and trim the very ends of the stalks. Drizzle with olive oil and season with salt and pepper.

Dampen the rosemary stalks with a little water and throw them onto the charcoal. Place the mushrooms gill-side up on the grill in the direct heat zone and divide half the butter between the mushroom cups, then close the lid of the barbecue. Cook for 5 minutes, then check to see if the mushrooms are cooked through; this will depend on their size – larger ones may need another minute or so.

Transfer the cooked mushrooms to the perimeter of the indirect heat zone. Divide the remaining butter evenly between them and leave for a minute or two to let the butter melt before serving.

Serves 4

100g (½ cup) unsalted butter, softened

2 garlic cloves, finely chopped

3 rosemary sprigs, leaves chopped, stalks reserved

8–12 portobello or flat-cap meaty mushrooms, stalks intact

2 tsp dark soy sauce

olive oil, for cooking

sea salt and black pepper

Italian-style seasonal greens with garlic, chilli and lemon

This is actually one of my favourites: a selection of vibrant seasonal greens tossed in good olive oil with a kick of garlic and chilli and a burst of lemon. You can vary the greens, but spinach, sprouting broccoli, chard and kale make for an interesting and delicious mix. Serve this hot, as the Italians do, or cold as a salad.

On the stovetop, bring a large pan of salted water to the boil. Check through the greens and trim any stalks as necessary. If you are using broccoli, cut the stalks into thin-ish strips that will cook in the same time as the leafy greens.

Fill a sink or large bowl with iced water, ready for refreshing the vegetables after blanching. In two batches, plunge the vegetables into the boiling water and cook for 2–3 minutes, then use tongs or a strainer to transfer them to the iced water. When the greens have completely cooled, drain well, squeezing gently to extract any excess water.

If you are making the cold salad, place the greens in a bowl with the garlic, chilli, lemon zest and juice, and season well. Drizzle in the extra virgin olive oil and toss before serving.

If you are serving the greens hot, heat a large sauté pan over low heat and add a lug of olive oil. Add the garlic and chilli and cook slowly for a minute or so to soften. Add the greens, stirring well to coat in the oil and heat through without crisping or colouring the leaves. Season, then stir in the lemon zest and juice. Serve immediately.

Serves 4

500g (18oz) mixed seasonal greens, such as cavolo nero, kale, chard, turnip tops, sprouting broccoli
ice
2 garlic cloves, finely chopped
2 red chillies, deseeded and thinly sliced
finely grated zest and juice of 1 lemon
50ml (3½ Tbsp) extra virgin olive oil – if serving as a salad
olive oil, for cooking
sea salt and black pepper

Charcoal-grilled chicory
with pomegranate molasses

I find chicory (or Belgian endive) to be much-underrated. It is generally used raw in salads –which is no bad thing – but cooked over charcoal, it is a revelation. I think it's something to do with the layers of leaves being exposed to charring and the natural bitterness being tempered. Sweet, sticky pomegranate molasses is the perfect accompaniment.

Light the barbecue and set for direct cooking.

Cut each head of chicory into quarters lengthwise. The yellow chicory will likely be bigger with a thicker stalk, so trim any excess stalk before cooking.

Rub the chicory with olive oil, season well and then place on the grill in the direct heat zone and cook for 3 minutes on each side to soften and char. Don't be afraid to blacken the leaves here – chicory really benefits from this depth of flavour.

When the chicory has softened, you should be able to splay out the leaves like a fan. Cook like this for a further 2 minutes on each side. Drizzle with the pomegranate molasses before serving.

Serves 4

4 heads red chicory
3 heads white chicory
2 Tbsp pomegranate molasses
olive oil, for cooking
sea salt and black pepper

Charcoal-baked potato and fresh herb gnocchi

A great way to cook baked potatoes is to nestle them among the coals you're using to barbecue something else until the skin crisps and the flesh is soft and tender. This slow charcoal-baking really intensifies the potato flavour, and gives gnocchi made from them a distinctive smokiness. With plenty of fresh herbs and a final tossing with smoked butter or pan-frying in olive oil, these gnocchi make a great accompaniment to lighter dishes.

Light the barbecue and set for direct cooking.

Prick the potatoes all over with a fork, then wrap them individually in foil, adding a good sprinkle of sea salt. Nestle the potatoes among the hot coals and close the lid of the barbecue. Cook for 1½ hours or until the potatoes are tender and soft – the skin will be crisp, so insert a small knife into the flesh to check it's done.

Remove the potatoes from the barbecue and when they are just cool enough to handle, scoop out the potato flesh and press it through a potato ricer or masher into a bowl. (Eat the potato skins as a snack with some alioli – delicious!)

While the potato flesh is still warm, mix in the sifted flour and eggs to form a dough. The consistency should be similar to bread dough; if it feels too wet, add a touch more flour. Season with salt and pepper and mix in the herbs.

Bring a large pan of salted water to the boil on the stovetop, then turn down to a simmer. Take a small piece of gnocchi dough and drop it into the water. After a minute or so, it should rise to the surface, which indicates it is cooked. Scoop it out with a slotted spoon and taste, then adjust the seasoning of the rest of the gnocchi dough if needed.

Dust a tray or chopping board with flour. If you're using a piping bag, scrape the dough into it, then cut off the end to a make an opening about the width of a thumb and pipe the dough onto the tray or board in two or three lengths. Alternatively, just roll the dough by hand. Cut the lengths of dough into 2cm (¾in) gnocchi with a sharp knife, then slide them all into the simmering water to cook.

When the gnocchi have all risen to the surface, drain well. Either transfer to a bowl and toss with the smoked butter and a little more seasoning, or spread them out on a tray to cool before dusting with a little flour and pan-frying over medium heat in olive oil until golden brown.

Serves 4

A plastic piping bag is handy here

1kg (2¼lb) Desiree potatoes

200g (1½ cups) plain (all-purpose) flour, sifted

2 eggs, lightly beaten

2 Tbsp chopped fresh herbs, such as parsley, dill, mint, tarragon

50g (3½ Tbsp) Smoked butter (see page 244), or a lug of olive oil

sea salt and black pepper

Wood-roasted potatoes with thyme and garlic

These potatoes are simmered with lots of garlic and thyme to infuse them with flavour, then roasted over hot charcoal and oak wood chips with more garlic and thyme. This wonderful dish is brilliant straight from the grill with barbecued or roast chicken.

Place the potatoes in a medium saucepan, cover with cold water and add the halved garlic bulb and 3 of the thyme sprigs. Bring to the boil on the stovetop and cook until tender. Drain well and leave to cool, then cut the cooled potatoes into bite-size chunks.

Light the barbecue and set for direct/indirect cooking. Throw a good handful of wood chips onto the coals, if you like.

Take a roasting tin or ovenproof frying pan large enough to hold the potatoes and place in the direct heat zone. Add a good lug of olive oil and, when the oil starts to smoke, add the potatoes and season well. Toss the potatoes in the oil to coat, then close the lid of the barbecue.

Cook for 4 minutes before tossing the potatoes again and adding another handful of wood chips, if using. Cook for a further 3 minutes, then add the butter, extra garlic cloves and the leaves from the remaining 3 thyme sprigs. Toss the potatoes again, then transfer to the indirect heat zone and cook for 2 minutes, or until they are crisp and golden brown.

Serve the potatoes immediately, spooning over any butter, garlic and thyme left in the tin or pan.

Serves 4

You'll also need some beech or oak chips, if you want an extra-smoky flavour

800g (1¾lb) Charlotte, Pink Fir Apple or other waxy potatoes

1 garlic bulb, cut in half, plus 4 extra garlic cloves, peeled

6 sprigs thyme

50g (3½ Tbsp) unsalted butter

olive oil, for cooking

sea salt and black pepper

Seasonal salad of heritage carrots, organic leaves, radish and cumin dressing

I love using heritage carrots. Their interesting shapes and colours make for an exciting presentation, and cooking the carrots in a foil parcel helps retain all their natural sweetness and flavour. You can of course use bunched organic carrots or any other tasty organic variety. The cumin dressing is an unusual but highly successful pairing.

Light the barbecue and set for direct/indirect cooking.

Spread out a double layer of foil large enough to enclose the carrots. Place the carrots on the foil, then dot with the butter and add a drizzle of olive oil. Scatter over the garlic and 1 tablespoon of the cumin seeds, then season well before wrapping up the foil to make a well-sealed parcel.

Using long-handled tongs, nestle the parcel into the coals and cook for about 35–45 minutes, depending on the thickness of the carrots. When they are ready, they should be nice and tender. Carefully remove the parcel from the barbecue, then leave to rest and cool for 15 minutes.

Meanwhile, use a pestle and mortar or spice grinder to coarsely crush the remaining cumin seeds. Finely slice the radishes and place in a bowl, along with the salad leaves. Cut the carrots into small chunks or slices and add to the bowl.

Whisk together the honey, vinegar and extra virgin olive oil to make a dressing, then stir in the crushed cumin seeds.

Pour the dressing over the salad and toss well, mixing in any carrot tops. Season before serving.

Serves 4

1.2kg (2¾lb) mixed heritage or bunched organic carrots, stalks removed (save any feathery tops for the salad), washed
50g (3½ Tbsp) unsalted butter
3 garlic cloves, crushed
1½ Tbsp cumin seeds
50g (2oz) French Breakfast or White Icicle radishes, trimmed
2 handfuls of mixed salad leaves, washed
1½ Tbsp blossom honey
1½ Tbsp red wine vinegar
1½ Tbsp extra virgin olive oil
olive oil, for cooking
sea salt and black pepper

Roasted buttermilk parsnips with manchego and rosemary

Parsnips are one of my favourite root vegetables, as they're incredibly versatile and delicious. This is a take on *poutine*, the French-Canadian mélange of chips with grilled cheese and other bits and bobs, but I've given it a Spanish twist with manchego. The real revelation, though, is cooking the parsnips in buttermilk – not only does it give the parsnips a rich, slightly acidic flavour, but also the curds separate and turn into nuggets of deliciousness when roasted on the barbecue. A final flourish of truffle honey might be considered an indulgent step too far by some. I disagree.

Cut the parsnips into long thin strips about the size of French fries. Place the parsnip 'chips' in a medium saucepan and pour over the buttermilk and milk. Add some salt, then place the pan over medium heat on the stovetop. Bring to the boil, then turn down to a simmer and cook until the parsnips are nice and tender. Drain the parsnips and spread out on a tray or plate to cool – you'll notice little nuggets of curd on the parsnips that will cook to crispy delights!

Light the barbecue and set for direct cooking.

Place the parsnips in a roasting tin or large ovenproof frying pan – ideally one that will accommodate them in a single layer – then drizzle generously with olive oil and season well. Place the tin or pan on the barbecue and roast the parsnips for about 18–20 minutes, stirring occasionally to ensure they don't burn. You want the parsnips to be golden brown, and the curds deeper brown and crispy. If they need longer, close the lid of the barbecue and cook for a few more minutes, then check them again. When the parsnips are done, sprinkle over the cheese and rosemary and toss well, then give them another minute, with the lid closed, for the cheese to brown.

Remove the parsnips from the barbecue, immediately drizzle with the honey and sprinkle on a little more salt. I like to serve this in the tin or pan, so people can help themselves – just be sure to put a cloth underneath before putting it on the table!

Serves 4

600g (1lb 5oz) parsnips, peeled
400ml (1¾ cups) buttermilk
400ml (1¾ cups) full-cream (whole) milk
40g (½ cup) grated manchego cheese
2 tsp finely chopped rosemary leaves
4 Tbsp honey, ideally truffle honey
olive oil, for cooking
sea salt and black pepper

Ember-cooked beetroot with horseradish pickle

This is partially inspired by my Jewish grandmother, Ada, who passed away at the grand old age of 103. She came from a strict Jewish background, and she was a fantastic cook. One of her classics was a beetroot and horseradish pickle called *chraine*, which she served with everything from fried fish to roasts and cold meats, and everything in-between. I've cooked the beetroot in embers to put my twist on it, and added some caraway, but the memory of Ada's repertoire lives on!

Light the barbecue and set for direct cooking.

Wrap the beetroot individually in foil, adding a splash of olive oil, some salt and pepper and a third of the caraway seeds to each one before sealing.

When the charcoal is ashen grey, use long-handled tongs to carefully nestle the beetroot parcels into the coals, burying them so they are completely covered. Cook for about 1 hour or until tender – a knife inserted into the beetroot should glide in without any resistance.

Leave the beetroot parcels to cool, then remove the foil and peel the skins; save the caraway seeds for the pickle blend. Roughly chop the beetroot, then transfer to a food processor, along with the horseradish, garlic, vinegar, sugar and salt, and the reserved roasted caraway seeds. Blend to a rough purée, then check the seasoning.

Transfer to a Kilner-style jar, then seal and leave to marinate for at least 2 hours in the fridge before using. The pickle will continue to improve and develop over time and will keep for up to 4 weeks in the fridge.

Serves 4 (makes about 475ml/ 2 cups)

- 3 medium beetroot, washed and stalks trimmed
- 1 tsp caraway seeds
- 1 x 7.5cm (3in) piece fresh horseradish, peeled and roughly chopped – or more if you like it really hot and punchy!
- 1 garlic clove, roughly chopped
- 3 Tbsp Cabernet Sauvignon vinegar or other red wine vinegar
- 1½ tsp caster (superfine) sugar
- 2 tsp fine salt
- olive oil, for cooking
- sea salt and black pepper

Grilled courgettes
with parmesan

Courgettes are wonderful grilled on the barbecue.
I find they can be a little watery and insipid at
times, but cooking them slowly over charcoal
intensifies the flavours and sweetens them to great
effect. Grating over some parmesan a minute or
so before they come off the grill adds a salty tang.
This makes a great accompaniment to pork and
chicken dishes.

Light the barbecue and set for direct/indirect cooking.

Sprinkle the courgettes with a little salt and let them sit for 20
minutes to extract any bitter juices and excess liquid.

Pat the courgettes dry, then drizzle them with olive oil and
place, cut-side down, on the grill over the direct heat zone and
char for 3 minutes, then turn over and cook for a further 3
minutes. The courgettes should be starting to soften by now.
Transfer them to the middle of the indirect heat zone and
close the lid of the barbecue. Cook for a further 3–4 minutes
to soften further and caramelize – this will sweeten the
courgettes and make them tastier. Just before they're ready,
sprinkle over the cheese and briefly close the lid again to melt
the cheese.

Serve with a little more sea salt – and a good drizzle of extra
virgin olive oil, if you like.

Serves 4

4 medium courgettes (zucchini),
  cut in half lengthwise
olive oil, for cooking
25g (⅓ cup) finely grated parmesan
sea salt and black pepper
good fruity extra virgin olive, for
  drizzling – optional

Slow-cooked carrots with cardamom and orange

Over the years, I've found that carrots go particularly well with exotic spices, and this dish of colourful carrots caramelized slowly over the grill and basted with a cardamom-and-orange-infused butter is a case in point. If this doesn't transport you to somewhere far-flung, hot and exciting, then nothing will! I love serving this with Grilled free-range chicken with yogurt, lemon and North-African spices (see page 157) or Slow-cooked hogget shoulder (see page 130).

Light the barbecue and set for direct/indirect cooking.

Over low heat on the stovetop, melt the butter in a small saucepan, then add the cardamom pods, the orange zest and half of the orange juice. Cook the butter very slowly for 5 minutes to infuse it with the cardamom and orange, then remove from the heat and reserve in a warm spot.

Wash the carrots and give them a little scrub if needed, but don't peel them. Rub with olive oil and season, then place the carrots on the grill in the direct heat zone. Cook for 5 minutes, turning regularly, until the carrots have charred and started to caramelize.

Now brush the carrots all over with some of the infused butter and move them to the indirect heat zone. Cook for 4 minutes, then brush with more of the butter. Repeat twice more until the carrots are glazed, tender and nicely caramelized. Squeeze over the rest of the orange juice and serve straightaway.

Serves 4

100g (½ cup) unsalted butter
6 cardamom pods, crushed
grated zest and juice of 1 large orange
800g (1¾ lb) mixed heritage or
  regular carrots
olive oil, for cooking
sea salt and black pepper

Smoked mashed potato

This wickedly naughty mash comes with the added bonus of smokiness from oak-smoked milk and cream – it works a treat and adds a natural sweetness to the potatoes. My favourite potato for mashing is the red-skinned Desiree as it has firm, creamy flesh that doesn't absorb too much water on cooking; Maris Piper makes a good substitute.

Set up the cold-smoking device in the barbecue with the oak chips and get it going, then place the grill rack on top.

Pour the cream and milk into a medium bowl, then place on the rack and close the lid and vent of the barbecue. Cold-smoke for 1 hour, then remove the bowl from the barbecue and leave to rest for 1 hour.

Cut the potatoes into even chunks, then place in a saucepan and cover with cold water. Season with salt. Bring to the boil on the stovetop, then simmer until the potatoes are nice and tender. Drain, then return the potatoes to the hot pan and let them steam-dry for 2 minutes.

Mash the potatoes or press through a potato ricer or masher into a bowl. Pour in the smoked cream and milk and stir in the butter. Season to taste, then serve immediately.

Serves 4

You'll also need a cold-smoking device and some oak chips

100ml (generous ⅓ cup) double (heavy) cream

75ml (⅓ cup) full-cream (whole) milk

600g (1lb 5oz) Desiree potatoes, peeled

50g (3½ Tbsp) unsalted butter, diced

sea salt and white pepper

Creamy white polenta with fennel seeds and chilli

A heart-warming bowl of smooth creamy polenta infused with aromatic fennel seeds and spiked with chilli, this cries out to be paired with something braised or slow-cooked. It's the ultimate Italian-style, winter comfort food. If you prefer, you can use yellow or instant polenta – just remember to adjust the cooking time accordingly.

Pour 750ml (3¼ cups) of the milk into a medium saucepan and season. Place over medium heat on the stovetop and bring to the boil, then pour in the polenta in a steady steam and whisk until fully incorporated. Turn the heat down to low and cook slowly for about 30 minutes, stirring regularly.

While the polenta is cooking, heat a lug of olive oil in a heavy-based frying pan and slowly fry the fennel seeds, fresh chilli and chilli flakes for 2–3 minutes, just to release their natural oils.

When the polenta is nearly ready, whisk in the cheese and butter, along with the fennel and chilli oil. Check the seasoning and adjust as necessary. If the polenta seems too thick, whisk in the rest of the milk. Serve immediately.

Serves 4–6

750–900ml (3¼–4 cups) full-cream (whole) milk
250g (1½ cups) white polenta
1 Tbsp fennel seeds
½ fresh red chilli, finely chopped
¼ tsp dried chilli flakes
30g (½ cup) finely grated parmesan
25g (1½ Tbsp) unsalted butter
olive oil, for cooking
sea salt and black pepper

DESSERTS

Admittedly, barbecues aren't generally associated with desserts, but all the more reason to show you what you can do.

When I decided to write this book, I talked to a few of my friends and colleagues about it and, happily, everyone thought it was a great idea. However, one subject that kept cropping up was desserts – or puddings, as I still like to call them. It seemed like a bit of a cop-out to just tack a list of sweet treats on to the end of the book that had no connection to barbecuing. So the only thing to do was create some delicious, mouth-watering puddings that involved the lick of an open flame or the aroma of smoke. I hope this puts the doubters firmly back in their place!

Most things you can do in an oven you can do on the barbecue, given a bit of know-how. Softer fruit, such as strawberries, figs and plums, work particularly well cooked directly over hot charcoal, as their natural sugars caramelize into jammy heaven. Harder fruit, such as apples and pears, require a little longer on the barbecue or in the coals but benefit all the more for that; wrapping them in a protective foil jacket while they slowly bake shields the fruit from the fiery heat while also helping them to cook more evenly.

I urge you to try the smoked-milk ice cream, which was inspired by one of my food jaunts to the Spanish Basque Country, where I had a memorable meal at Asador Etxebarri. The chef there, Victor Arguinzoniz, is a genius, producing refined grilled food that is consistently sublime. The puddings are always seasonal, made by treating the very best local produce very simply, with just a little twist of smokiness to enhance, rather than mask, its taste.

The chocolate recipes proved really interesting: I've discovered that cocoa butter takes on smokiness really well. However, the resulting complexity of flavour is difficult to sum up in words, so I'm afraid you'll just have to get cooking and eating – you'll soon understand what I mean! In case you develop a taste for smoke with your chocolate, I've also included a recipe for cold-smoking your own chocolate (see page 248), so you can experiment with using it in other recipes, or just have a bar or two around to munch on. It's dangerously addictive stuff.

All the recipes in this section are straightforward to prepare and cook. There are no perplexing techniques; just simple cooking and fantastic flavours. It may have become somewhat of a cliché now, but it's still so very true: when you have fantastic ingredients, you don't need to mess around with them – let them sing.

Chargrilled pineapple with yogurt mousse and pistachio praline

There's nothing like pineapple to transport you to exotic climes and holidays in the sun. Here, the fruit's naturally sweet juices are caramelized over charcoal with the aid of a vanilla basting syrup. The yogurt mousse makes a delicious, fresh-tasting foil for the rich pineapple, and crunch comes from a scattering of praline flecked with green pistachios.

Trim the top and bottom from the pineapple, then stand it upright on a board and use a long sharp knife to cut away the skin. Cut the pineapple into quarters lengthwise, then trim away the central core from each piece before cutting into 6 slices. Lay the slices on a paper-towel-lined tray or plate in the fridge for an hour to dry a little.

Next make the yogurt mousse. Drain the gelatine from the water and squeeze out any excess. In a small saucepan on the stovetop, gently heat 50g (¼ cup) of the yogurt until it is very warm (but don't let it get too hot or it may split), then whisk in the gelatine. When the gelatine has completely dissolved, transfer to a medium bowl and whisk in the sugar and the remaining yogurt. In a separate bowl, whip the cream to soft peaks, then fold this into the yogurt mix. Transfer to the fridge to set – this will take about 1 hour.

For the vanilla syrup, place the sugar in a small saucepan with 3½ tablespoons water. Scrape the seeds from the vanilla pod and add to the pan, along with the pod. Bring to the boil on the stovetop, then let it simmer for a few minutes until the sugar has dissolved. Remove from the heat and set aside.

For the pistachio praline, lightly oil a baking sheet. Place the sugar in a small heavy-based saucepan with 3½ tablespoons water and cook over medium heat on the stovetop, shaking the pan every now and then until it melts into a caramel and turns a deep golden brown. Don't stir it, or the sugar might crystallize. Throw in the pistachio nuts and shake the pan to coat them in the caramel, then carefully pour onto the prepared sheet and leave to cool completely. Transfer the praline to a clean tea towel, then cover and bash with a rolling pin or the heel of a knife to break it up. Ideally, you want some irregular shards, along with some more finely crushed pieces.

Light the barbecue and set for direct cooking.

Brush the pineapple slices with vanilla syrup, then place them directly on the grill and cook for 2 minutes to char before turning. Brush again with syrup and continue to cook and turn until the pineapple is evenly charred and very tender.

Brush the grilled pineapple with the syrup once more to glaze, then serve it with the mousse and praline on top.

Serves 4

1 medium pineapple

For the yogurt mousse
2 gelatine leaves, soaked in cold water for about 5 minutes
350g (1½ cups) thick, Greek-style yogurt
50g (¼ cup) caster (superfine) sugar
200ml (generous ¾ cup) double (heavy) cream

For the vanilla syrup
50g (¼ cup) caster (superfine) sugar
1 vanilla pod (bean), split

For the pistachio praline
100g (½ cup) caster (superfine) sugar
50g (⅓ cup) roughly chopped pistachios

Cherry and almond tart

This tart is great fun to make – and once you've mastered it, you've got a really versatile base to work with, varying the fruits with the seasons. Cherry and almond is a classic match, though, and this cries out for a glass of something sweet and strong, to wash it down with, such as a Frangelico or Amaretto.

Sitting the tart on a soaked wooden plank to cook in the barbecue protects its base from burning.

Grease the tin or pan with butter and dust with flour, then put in the fridge to chill. Place a large sheet of baking paper on a work surface and dust with sugar, then sit the pastry on top and cover with another sheet of baking paper. Roll out the pastry between the two sheets of paper to a thickness of about 3mm (⅛ in) and with a circumference large enough to line the tin with some overhang. Carefully transfer the pastry to the tin. Don't worry about any small holes or tears – just patch them up as best you can with a little of the excess overhanging pastry. Press the pastry into the base and sides of the tin, then prick the base all over with a fork. Cover the tart shell with a crumpled sheet of baking paper and refrigerate for 20 minutes.

Meanwhile, preheat the oven to 180°C (350°F).

Make a frangipane by creaming the butter and sugar until light and fluffy (either using an electric mixer or by hand), then beat in the eggs one by one. Finally, fold in the flour and almonds until fully incorporated.

Fill the lined tart shell with baking beans or uncooked rice, then blind bake for 10–15 minutes, or until the base and sides are cooked and crisp but still pale.

Light the barbecue and set for direct/indirect cooking. Place the lump of wood to the side of the charcoal to start smoking. (You want the temperature inside the barbecue to be about 180–190°C/350–375°F; regulate with the vents and lid during the baking time, if needed.)

Remove the tart shell from the oven, take out the paper and beans or rice and leave to cool for 10 minutes before cutting away the crust overhang with a small knife. Spoon the frangipane into the tart shell and dot the cherries on top.

Wrap the base and sides of the tin in a double layer of foil to help buffer the fierce heat rising from the coals. Sit the tart on the plank, then transfer to the indirect heat zone and close the lid of the barbecue. Cook the tart for 35–40 minutes or until the crust has browned, the frangipane has just set (a skewer inserted in the centre should come out fairly clean) and the cherries have started to bleed their juices.

Remove the tart from the barbecue and leave to cool for an hour before serving.

Serves 4

You'll also need a 20cm (8in) non-stick tart (flan) tin or frying pan, a lump of hardwood and a length of soaked wooden plank

1 quantity Sweet pastry (see page 247), at room temperature

125g (½ cup) unsalted butter, at room temperature, plus extra for greasing

125g (⅔ cup) caster (superfine) sugar, plus extra for dusting

3 free-range eggs

125g (scant 1 cup) plain (all-purpose) flour, sifted, plus extra for dusting

220g (1¾ cups) cherries, pitted

125g (1¼ cups) ground almonds (almond meal)

Smoked-milk ice cream with seasonal berries

This very unusual and intriguing recipe pairs smoky milk with berries of your choice. My particular favourites are blackberries and blueberries. I'm afraid there's a little trial and error involved when the milk meets the smoke. I tend to aim for a fairly faint background flavour that comes through at the end, as I feel that a strong, in-your-face smokiness can overwhelm sweeter things. Of course, it's all subjective, so have fun experimenting – just remember to allow time for the smoked milk to rest overnight.

First make the smoked-milk ice cream. Set up the cold-smoking device in the barbecue with the wood dust and get it going. Pour the milk into a wide heatproof bowl or tray and place in the barbecue, then close the lid and vent and leave to cold-smoke for 1 hour. Cover the bowl of smoked milk, then chill in the fridge overnight to rest and balance.

Next day, place the smoked milk and the sugar in a saucepan over low heat on the stovetop and carefully reduce by half – keep a close eye on it, as it can easily boil over. Pour into a bowl, then whisk in the condensed milk and leave to cool before transferring to an ice-cream machine and churning according to the manufacturer's instructions. (If you don't have an ice-cream machine, freeze the ice cream in a shallow container, whisking it every hour to break up the ice crystals until you are happy with the consistency.)

When the ice cream is ready, place the sugar, lemon zest and juice, along with 125ml (½ cup) water, in a non-reactive saucepan and bring to the boil. Remove from the heat and add all the berries, then cover the pan and leave for 15 minutes to macerate and cool slightly.

Divide the berries between the bowls and serve with a scoop of smoked-milk ice cream on top. Delicious!

Serves 4

You'll also need a cold-smoking device and some wood dust

125g (⅔ cup) caster (superfine) sugar
finely grated zest and juice of 1 lemon
400g (14oz) mixed seasonal berries, such as blueberries, blackberries, small strawberries, raspberries, redcurrants

For the smoked-milk ice cream
500ml (generous 2 cups) full-cream (whole) milk
15g (1 Tbsp) caster (superfine) sugar
70ml (5 Tbsp) condensed milk

Grilled strawberries with mascarpone and black pepper

An unusual dessert maybe, but a really quick and delicious one. The spicy black pepper really heightens the sweetness of the strawberries. For the best flavour, buy local strawberries for this, and choose ones that aren't over-ripe. If they're too soft, you might end up with barbecued strawberry jam!

Light the barbecue and set for direct cooking.

Hull the strawberries and cut in half lengthwise. Spread them out on a tray or plate, cut-side up, and chill in the fridge for 20 minutes to dry the surface.

Whisk the mascarpone with the icing sugar and a grinding or pinch of black pepper. Set aside in the fridge.

Using a sieve or dredger, dust some icing sugar over the strawberries, then place them cut-side down on the grill. Cook for 4 minutes to char before carefully flipping them over and cooking for a further minute. The strawberries should still be a little firm, but the juices should have started bubbling from them.

Transfer the hot strawberries to a serving platter, drizzle over the balsamic vinegar and grind over 3 turns of the pepper mill or 2 pinches of black pepper.

Leave the strawberries for 10 minutes to macerate and then serve along with the balsamic-strawberry juices and a dollop of the mascarpone.

Serves 4

250g (2½ cups) large strawberries
150g (⅔ cup) mascarpone
40g (¼ cup) icing (confectioners') sugar, plus extra for dusting
about ½ tsp freshly ground black pepper
25ml (1½ Tbsp) balsamic vinegar

Smoked-chocolate salami with shortbread, almonds and raisins

This is my take on the chocolate 'salami' found across Italy and Portugal, which resembles – in looks only – the cured meat sausage of the same name. This keeps well in the fridge and is great brought out at the end of dinner, to be enjoyed with some coffee and a digestif.

Pour the cream into a small saucepan and bring to a simmer on the stovetop. Place the chocolate in a heatproof bowl and pour the cream over, then stir well until the chocolate has melted and the mixture is smooth and glossy.

Drain the raisins and add to the chocolate. Roughly chop the almonds and the shortbread and add these to the chocolate as well, mixing to fully incorporate.

Transfer to the fridge and chill for about 40 minutes until the mixture has started to firm up and is malleable.

On a work surface, lay out two large sheets of cling film. Spoon the mixture onto the centre of the cling film, then use your hands to shape it into a log. Fold both layers of the cling film over the log, then roll up as tightly as possible to create a tight, compact cylinder, without any gaps in the cling film. Tie the ends of the chocolate 'salami' with string and leave in the fridge for at least 1 hour to chill and rest.

Bring the salami back to room temperature before slicing and then serving.

Makes a 700g (1lb 8oz) log that will serve about 10 people

- 250ml (generous 1 cup) double (heavy) cream
- 250g (9oz) Smoked bitter chocolate (see page 248)
- 30g (¼ cup) raisins, soaked in a little warm water for about 15 minutes
- 50g (⅓ cup) Marcona almonds or blanched almonds
- 100g (3½oz) good-quality all-butter shortbread biscuits

Smoky rice pudding with pomegranate molasses

The perfect winter pudding, or indeed an indulgent breakfast! Rice pudding has its roots firmly in comfort-pudding territory, but sometimes it can be a little too stodgy. My version is quite light, and the pomegranate molasses adds a sweet-sour tang to cut through the sweet, milky pudding. I like to use Spanish Calasparra rice for a great, nutty texture – it's available in some supermarkets and online. But, failing that, a good-quality short-grain pudding rice will do well.

Light the barbecue and set for direct/indirect cooking. Add the lump of wood to the ashen charcoal to start smoking.

Combine all the ingredients, except the pomegranate molasses, in the dish. Place in the indirect heat zone, close the lid of the barbecue and cook slowly for 30 minutes. Top up with about 200ml (¾ cup) of water and stir well before cooking for a further 30 minutes. When it is ready the pudding should be thick and creamy and the rice grains just tender.

Serve the rice pudding immediately, drizzled with pomegranate molasses.

Serves 6

You'll also need a sturdy, heavy-based ovenproof saucepan or ceramic dish and a lump of hardwood

300g (1½ cups) Calasparra rice or short-grain pudding rice

1 vanilla pod (bean), split and seeds removed

2 cinnamon sticks

zest of 1 orange, peeled off in fine strips

zest of 1 lemon, peeled off in strips

175g (1 cup) caster (superfine) sugar

1.5L (6¼ cups) full-cream (whole) milk

2 Tbsp pomegranate molasses

Barbecued apples with muscovado, raisins, pine nuts and clotted cream

These are fantastic served directly from the barbecue in their foil jackets, but let them cool a bit first so you're not juggling them around! I like to cook these apples during the winter months – they're great for a bonfire-night or Thanksgiving gathering, especially with some hot, mulled cider to wash them down.

Light the barbecue and set for direct/indirect cooking.

Pour the sherry over the raisins, then mix in 75g (⅓ cup) of the muscovado sugar and the lemon zest. Lightly toast the pine nuts over a low heat in a small frying pan until golden brown. Leave to cool, then chop roughly and add to the raisin mixture.

Remove the cores from the apples using a corer or small knife – you want to create a cavity right through the middle of the apple to stuff. Lay out 4 sheets of foil, each large enough to wrap an apple well, then sit an apple on each one. Stuff the cavities generously with the raisin mixture; if a little spills down the sides, that's fine. Top the apples with the remaining muscovado sugar and dot with the butter, then wrap them up tightly so they are well sealed.

Place the apples in the indirect heat zone and close the lid (the temperature inside the barbecue should be about 170°C/340°F). Cook for about 40 minutes, until the apples are soft to the touch, rotating them a couple of times to ensure they cook evenly.

Remove from the barbecue and leave to cool for 5 minutes. Meanwhile, whisk the clotted cream with the icing sugar to combine. Open the foil, top the apples with the sweetened cream and serve.

Serves 4

50ml (3½ Tbsp) sweet, syrupy sherry, such as Pedro Ximénez
50g (⅓ cup) raisins
100g (½ cup) dark muscovado sugar
finely grated zest of 1 lemon
50g (⅓ cup) pine nuts
4 large Cox's Orange Pippin apples
25g (1½ Tbsp) unsalted butter
150g (⅔ cup) clotted (heavy) cream
30g (¼ cup) icing (confectioners') sugar, sifted

Smoky bitter-chocolate puddings with melting whipped cream

This is my go-to dessert when indulgence is the order of the day. You can't help being seduced by molten chocolate with a light smoky edge, served with some cooling rich cream. There are always oohs and ahhs when these are served – and to think you cooked them on the barbecue too!

Grease the inside of each ramekin with the extra butter, then dust with the extra sugar.

Place the chocolate and butter in a large heatproof bowl and melt slowly over a pan of simmering water, making sure the base of the bowl isn't touching the water. Once melted, leave to cool slightly.

In a separate bowl, whisk together the eggs, egg yolks and sugar until light, fluffy and pale (an electric whisk is ideal for this), then fold into the melted chocolate mixture. Finally, fold in the flour as gently as possible.

Divide the mixture evenly between the prepared ramekins, then chill in the fridge for 30 minutes.

Meanwhile, whip the cream to just beyond soft peaks, so it will hold its shape when spooned on top of the hot puddings.

Light the barbecue and set for direct/indirect cooking (the temperature inside the barbecue should be about 180°C/350°F). Place the puddings in the indirect heat zone, close the lid and cook for 7 minutes. The puddings should have risen like a soufflé, have a light crust and still be molten in the centre.

Use a small spoon to carefully break the crust on top, then add a dollop of the whipped cream and serve immediately.

Serves 4

You'll also need 4 ramekins or other ovenproof dishes, 5cm (2in) deep and 9cm (3½in) in diameter

75g (2¾oz) Smoked bitter chocolate (see page 248)

60g (¼ cup) unsalted butter, plus extra for the ramekins

2 whole free-range eggs

2 free-range egg yolks

70g (⅓ cup) caster (superfine) sugar, plus extra for dusting the ramekins

30g (scant ¼ cup) plain (all-purpose) flour, sifted

150g (⅔ cup) double (heavy) cream

Charcoal-grilled peaches with lavender honey and mascarpone ice cream

This is a real favourite of mine, inspired by summer travels in northern Spain. Charred, smoky peaches with a light, cooling ice cream and the fragrance of lavender make for a beautiful, contrasting combination.

First make the mascarpone ice cream. Pour the cream and milk into a saucepan and bring to a simmer on the stovetop. In a heatproof bowl, whisk together the egg yolks and sugar until pale and fluffy. Pour over a third of the cream and milk, whisking to incorporate, then slowly whisk in the remainder. Pour the mixture back into the saucepan and cook over low heat, stirring constantly until smooth and thickened – when it's ready, the custard should coat the back of a spoon. Pour into a bowl and leave to cool for 5 minutes before whisking in the mascarpone.

Transfer to an ice-cream machine and churn according to the manufacturer's instructions. (If you don't have an ice-cream machine, freeze the ice cream in a shallow container, whisking it every hour to break up the ice crystals, until you are happy with the consistency.)

Cut the peaches in half, remove the stone and then cut each half again so you get four round slices from each peach. Lay the slices on a paper-towel-lined tray or plate in the fridge for 30 minutes to dry a little.

Light the barbecue and set for direct cooking. Throw the wood chips onto the coals, then lay the peach slices on the grill and close the lid of the barbecue.

Cook the peach slices for 5 minutes before turning them over and cooking for a further 3 minutes – they should be soft and well charred.

Meanwhile, take the ice cream from the freezer to let it soften slightly.

Transfer the peaches to a serving platter, drizzle over the honey and sprinkle with the lavender flowers, if you're using them, then serve with the ice cream.

Serves 4

You'll also need a handful of wood chips

4 firm peaches
100ml (⅓ cup) lavender honey
1 tsp dried lavender flowers – optional

For the mascarpone ice cream
150ml (⅔ cup) double (heavy) cream
250ml (generous 1 cup) full-cream (whole) milk
5 free-range egg yolks
75g (⅓ cup) caster (superfine) sugar
100g (scant ½ cup) mascarpone

Caramelized oranges with orange flower yogurt and honeycomb

When they are in season, I like to use ruby-tinged blood oranges for this, but you can use any oranges with a good flavour. Orange flower water is a by-product of the distillation of fresh orange blossom for its essential oil. Used for many years in Mediterranean and Middle Eastern cuisine, just a few intense drops add an exotic, almost otherworldly taste and aroma. This makes more honeycomb than you need here, but it will keep for a few days and is great added to any dessert to give it a sweet-caramel crunch, or eaten as a snack.

First make the honeycomb. Lightly grease a baking sheet. Place the sugar, glucose, honey and a tablespoon of water in a medium-sized saucepan and cook over high heat on the stovetop until the mixture turns golden brown. Immediately add the bicarbonate of soda and give it three sharp whisks – the honeycomb will rapidly expand and rise up like an erupting volcano. When this happens, give it another quick whisk then remove the pan from the heat and pour the frothing honeycomb onto the prepared sheet. Leave to settle and cool completely. The honeycomb will keep for up to a week in an airtight container (but don't put it in the fridge, or it will lose its crunch).

Light the barbecue and set for direct cooking.

Slice the top and bottom off each orange, then sit it on a chopping board. Using a sharp paring knife, carefully cut away all the skin and pith from the oranges, then slice each one into 4 even rounds. Dust with sugar, then place on the grill and cook for 3 minutes either side until charred and tender.

Meanwhile, place the sugar and 200ml (generous ¾ cup) of water in a large non-stick frying pan. Heat on the barbecue, without stirring, until you have a deep-brown caramel. Carefully transfer the oranges to the pan and move it to the edge of the barbecue to cook slowly for 5 minutes or until the oranges are syrupy, soft and delicious. Remove from the heat but leave the oranges to cool in the syrup.

Whisk the yogurt with the orange flower water and serve with the oranges. Drizzle with some of the syrup and strew some chunks of honeycomb over the top.

Serves 4

4 small oranges, such as blood oranges, or 2 large navel oranges
200g (1 cup) caster (superfine) sugar, plus extra for dusting
150g (¾ cup) thick Greek yogurt
1 tsp orange flower water

For the honeycomb
100g (½ cup) caster (superfine) sugar
35g (4 tsp) liquid glucose
20g (3 tsp) honey
1 tsp bicarbonate of soda (baking soda)

Walnut and coffee cake with salted caramel and clotted cream

The flavours and textures in this dessert tick all the boxes for me and work incredibly well together. Who doesn't like salted caramel?! You'll need to monitor the temperature of the barbecue quite closely and use the top vents to regulate the heat as necessary.

Mix the coffee with a splash of boiling water to form a thick syrup, then leave to cool. Place the walnut halves in a small frying pan and lightly toast over low–medium heat on the stovetop until they smell nutty. Allow to cool slightly, then roughly chop.

Light the barbecue and set for direct/indirect cooking (you want the temperature inside the barbecue to be a fairly constant 210–220°C/410–425°F).

Grease the loaf pan and line the base with baking paper.

Either using an electric mixer or by hand, cream together the butter and sugar until light and airy. Gradually add the beaten eggs, mixing constantly, until incorporated. Sift in the flour, baking powder and salt, then gently fold in with a spoon. Finally, fold in the coffee syrup and two-thirds of the walnuts. Spoon the mixture into the prepared pan carefully and cleanly – try to avoid getting any drips on the side of the pan, as this can affect the cooking of the cake.

Place the lump of hardwood to the side of the ashen coals to start smoking.

Wrap a double layer of foil around the bottom half of the pan to help the fierce heat rising from the coals. Place the pan on the plank, then transfer to the indirect heat zone and close the lid of the barbecue. Cook the cake for 1 hour and 10 minutes, monitoring the heat as you go: the temperature should be about 210–220°C (410–425°F), but will fall to around 160°C (325°F) towards the end of the cooking time. This is fine – in fact, it finishes the cake nicely. Check that the cake is done by inserting a thin knife into the centre; it should come out fairly clean – a few crumbs of cake mix residue is absolutely fine.

Remove the cake from the barbecue and cool in the pan for 10 minutes before turning out onto a wire rack and leaving for 30 minutes to cool completely.

Meanwhile, whisk the cream with the icing sugar.

Cut the cake horizontally through the middle and spoon in the clotted cream. Sandwich the two halves together, then pour over as much of the salted caramel as you like and sprinkle over the remaining walnuts. Serve immediately.

<u>Serves about 8</u>

You'll also need a 22cm (8¾in) loaf pan, a lump of hardwood and a length of soaked wooden plank

2 Tbsp good-quality instant coffee

100g (¾ cup) walnut halves

225g (1 cup) unsalted butter, at room temperature

225g (1 cup, firmly packed) soft brown sugar

4 free-range eggs, lightly beaten

225g (1¾ cups) plain (all-purpose) flour

3 tsp baking powder

pinch of salt

100g (½ cup) clotted (heavy) cream

30g (3½ Tbsp) icing (confectioners') sugar

1 quantity Salted caramel (see page 248)

Caramelized fig tart with cinnamon ice cream

A tarte Tatin by any other name, this uses sweet jammy figs and dark, rich muscovado sugar. There's plenty of good-quality, readymade puff pastry out there – just make sure it's the all-butter variety, so it will be properly flaky and rich.

First make the ice cream. Place the milk, cream, cinnamon stick and ground cinnamon in a saucepan and bring slowly to the boil on the stovetop. Simmer for 5 minutes, then leave to cool for 5 minutes before discarding the cinnamon stick.

Meanwhile, in a heatproof bowl, whisk together the egg yolks and sugar until pale and fluffy. Pour over a third of the cinnamon-infused milk and cream, whisking to incorporate, then slowly whisk in the remainder. Pour back into the pan and cook over low heat, stirring constantly, until smooth and thickened – the custard should coat the back of a spoon.

Transfer to an ice-cream machine and churn according to the manufacturer's instructions. (If you don't have an ice-cream machine, freeze the ice cream in a shallow container, whisking it every hour to break up the ice crystals, until you are happy with the consistency.)

Light and set a barbecue for direct/indirect cooking and place the lump of wood onto the ashen coals to start smoking.

On a sheet of baking paper, roll out the puff pastry into a rough circle about 3mm (⅛ in) thick. Prick the pastry all over with a fork, then chill in the fridge for 30 minutes.

Lay the sliced butter in the pan and sprinkle over the sugar. Arrange the figs on top, cut-side down, pressing them down a little so they are snug in the pan. Insert the cinnamon stick among the figs and grate over the lemon zest.

Set the pan of figs on the grill in the direct heat zone and close the lid of the barbecue. Cook for 8 minutes or until the sugar has turned a deep caramel colour and the juices have just started to bleed from the figs. Remove the pan from the barbecue and leave to cool for 5 minutes before laying the pastry on top of the figs. Tuck the edges of the pastry down between the sides of the pan and the figs, then brush the top with the beaten egg. Place in the indirect heat zone of the barbecue and close the lid. Cook for 30 minutes until the pastry is crisp and deep golden brown.

Remove from the barbecue and leave to cool for 5 minutes before carefully flipping the tart out onto a plate and serving hot with the cinnamon ice cream.

Serves 4–6

You'll also need a medium-size non-stick frying pan and a lump of hardwood

1 sheet ready-rolled puff pastry

20g (1 Tbsp) cold unsalted butter, thinly sliced

80g (⅓ cup) dark muscovado (brown) sugar

6 black figs, cut in half

1 cinnamon stick

finely grated zest of ½ lemon

1 free-range egg, lightly beaten

For the cinnamon ice cream

250ml (generous 1 cup) full-cream (whole) milk

250ml (generous 1 cup) double (heavy) cream

1 cinnamon stick

½ tsp ground cinnamon

8 free-range egg yolks

125g (⅔ cup) caster (superfine) sugar

Buttermilk pannacotta with grilled rhubarb

A lovely refreshing pudding, which puts a spin on the classic pannacotta by using sweet-acidic buttermilk and then adding some delicious, grilled, day-glow sticks of forced rhubarb. The charring of the rhubarb makes for a really interesting flavour contrast. If you can't get forced rhubarb, or it's out of season, then regular is fine – it will just need longer to cook.

First make the pannacotta. Place the cream and the vanilla seeds and pod in a saucepan and slowly bring to the boil on the stovetop. Remove the pan from the heat, then whisk in the caster sugar and the squeezed-out gelatine leaves until completely dissolved. Leave to cool for 10 minutes, then remove and discard the vanilla pod and whisk in the buttermilk. Divide the cream evenly between the moulds and place in the fridge to set for at least 3 hours.

Light the barbecue and set for direct cooking.

Place the orange zest, juice and brown sugar in a small saucepan. Bring to the boil on the stovetop and simmer for 5 minutes until syrupy.

Brush the rhubarb with the syrup, then place directly on the grill over the coals. Grill for 3 minutes, then turn over and brush again with the syrup. Cook for another 3 minutes until just starting to soften. Transfer to a tray or plate and pour over the remaining syrup.

To turn out the pannacottas, either flash a blowtorch around the outside of the moulds or quickly run hot water over them. Turn out onto individual plates, then serve with the rhubarb and the remaining syrup spooned over. Alternatively, serve in teacups if that's what you've used.

Serves 4

You'll also need 4 plastic dariole or pudding moulds, or small teacups

finely grated zest of ½ orange
100ml (generous ⅓ cup) orange juice
50g (¼ cup) dark brown sugar
200g (7oz) forced rhubarb, cut into 10cm (4in) lengths

For the pannacotta
300ml (1¼ cups) double (heavy) cream
1 vanilla pod (bean), split and deseeded
70g (⅓ cup) caster (superfine) sugar
2½ sheets of leaf gelatine, soaked in cold water for about 5 minutes until softened
300ml (1¼ cups) buttermilk

Caramel-glazed pears with Vin Santo ice cream

A spin on the Tuscan classic of pears poached in Vin Santo: whole pears cooked in caramel to soften, then glazed to golden perfection. I like to use Conference or Packham pears in early autumn as they hold their shape well through cooking. The ice cream can be made in the freezer without a machine, if required.

First make the Vin Santo ice cream. Pour the cream and milk into a saucepan and bring to a simmer on the stovetop. In a heatproof bowl, whisk together the egg yolks and sugar until pale and fluffy. Pour over a third of the cream and milk, whisking to incorporate, then slowly whisk in the remainder. Pour the mixture back into the saucepan and cook over low heat, stirring constantly until smooth and thickened – when it's ready, the custard should coat the back of a spoon.

Transfer to an ice-cream machine and churn according to the manufacturer's instructions. If you don't have an ice-cream machine, freeze the ice cream in a shallow container, whisking it every hour to break up the ice crystals, until you are happy with the consistency. When the ice cream is almost ready, churn (or whisk) in the Vin Santo to incorporate and freeze for at least 30 minutes before serving.

Light the barbecue and set for direct/indirect cooking.

Peel the pears, cut them in half lengthwise and then carefully cut out the core with a small knife. Pour the sugar into a medium frying pan, along with 150ml (⅔ cup) of water and place in the direct heat zone of the barbecue. Bring to the boil and cook until you have a golden-brown caramel. Carefully lay the pear halves, cut-side down, in the caramel, then move the pan to the indirect heat zone and close the lid of the barbecue. Cook the pear halves for 6 minutes, then turn them over and top up the pan with a tablespoon or two of water. Close the lid again and cook the pears for a further 5 minutes, then baste the pears with the caramel. When they are ready, they should be glazed with the caramel and quite tender.

Serve the pears in bowls with the caramel spooned over and the ice cream scooped on top.

Serves 4

4 large pears
150g (¾ cup) caster (superfine) sugar

For the Vin Santo ice cream
250ml (generous 1 cup) double (heavy) cream
250ml (generous 1 cup) full-cream (whole) milk
8 free-range egg yolks
125g (⅔ cup) caster (superfine) sugar
75ml (⅓ cup) Vin Santo

Goat's cheesecakes and slow-cooked plums with sherry

Everybody loves a cheesecake, right? This one is very light and uses an easy no-cook method. The goat's cheese adds an unusual grassy tang and is really delicious – just make sure it's a very light, soft-textured one. As the plums are cooked nice and slowly to the side of the charcoal, doused with sherry and infused with some wood smoke along the way, you can put them on just as you're finishing cooking your main-course dishes. Couldn't be easier.

For the biscuit base, crush the amaretto and digestive biscuits under a clean tea towel with a rolling pin, or pulse in a food processor; you want the crumbs to be imperfect and fairly rustic, though, so go easy with the food processor. Place the crumbs in a bowl and mix in the butter. Place the ring moulds on a tray and divide the crumb mixture between them, pressing it down with the back of a spoon so the bases are firm and level. Transfer to the fridge and chill for an hour.

For the cheesecake, whip the cream in a bowl until it forms stiff peaks. In a separate bowl, whisk together all the other ingredients – an electric mixer is good for this – until smooth and fully incorporated. Using a spatula or large metal spoon gently fold in the whipped cream. Spoon the cheesecake mixture into the moulds, tapping the outside of each ring to make sure the mixture settles into the mould, leaving no air gaps. Place the cheesecakes in the fridge for a couple of hours to set.

Light the barbecue and set for direct/indirect cooking. Place the lump of hardwood onto the ashen coals to smoke.

Place the plum halves, skin-side down, on the grill in the indirect heat zone of the barbecue and drizzle with some of the PX. Close the lid and cook for 10 minutes before drizzling with more PX and cooking for a further 10 minutes, still with the lid down. Finally, move the plums to the direct heat zone to char for 5 minutes, placing them skin-side up. Transfer to a tray or plate, drizzle over a little more PX and leave the plums to macerate for 20 minutes.

Carefully remove the cheesecakes from the moulds by warming the outside of the rings with a blowtorch or hot towel. Place on serving plates, along with the slow-cooked plums and syrupy PX juices.

Serves 6

You'll also need six 4.5cm (1¾in) ring moulds or individual tart tins, and a lump of hardwood

6 Victoria plums, cut in half and stones removed
100ml (⅓ cup plus 1 Tbsp) Pedro Ximénez (PX) sherry

For the biscuit base
150g (5½ oz) amaretti biscuits
85g (3oz) digestive biscuits (graham crackers)
85g (⅓ cup) unsalted butter, melted

For the cheesecake mixture
85ml (⅓ cup) double (heavy) cream
150g (⅔ cup) cream cheese
75g (⅓ cup) mascarpone
60g (¼ cup) caprini fresco or other soft, light, rindless goat's cheese
75g (⅓ cup) caster (superfine) sugar
seeds from ½ vanilla pod (bean)

Milk chocolate and grilled apricot tart

It's a joyous occasion when fresh apricots arrive in our markets. These little amber stone fruits epitomize the balmy days of late summer. They really showcase what the power of the sun can do to a fruit – the best apricots come from the warmer Mediterranean climes, and they should still feel firm to the touch when you buy them.

Grease the tart tin with butter and dust with flour, then put in the fridge to chill. Place a large sheet of non-stick baking paper on a work surface and dust with sugar, then sit the pastry on top and cover with another sheet of paper. Roll out the pastry between the sheets to a thickness of 3mm (⅛ in) and with a circumference large enough to line the tin with some overhang. Transfer the pastry to the tin. Don't worry about any small tears – patch them up with a little of the excess overhanging pastry. Press the pastry into the base and sides of the tin, then prick the base all over with a fork. Cover with a crumpled sheet of baking paper and refrigerate for 20 minutes.

Meanwhile, preheat the oven to 180°C (350°F).

Fill the lined tart shell with baking beans or uncooked rice, then blind bake for 10–15 minutes, or until the pastry is cooked and crisp but still pale. Remove the tart shell from the oven, take out the paper and beans/rice and cool for 10 minutes before cutting away the crust overhang with a knife.

Light the barbecue and set for direct/indirect cooking. Place the lumps of wood on the ashen charcoal to start smoking.

For the chocolate filling, place the chocolate in a large heatproof bowl and melt over a pan of simmering water (make sure the base of the bowl isn't touching the water), then whisk in the melted butter. Using an electric mixer, whisk the eggs and sugar in a separate bowl until pale, light and fluffy, then fold into the melted chocolate a third at a time.

Place the apricot halves, cut side down, on the grill in the direct heat zone of the barbecue and char for 3 minutes on each side. Arrange the apricots in the tart shell, then pour over the chocolate filling. Wrap the base and sides of the tin in 2 layers of foil to help buffer the fierce heat from the coals. Sit the tart on the plank, then transfer to the indirect heat zone and close the lid of the barbecue (you want the temperature inside to be about 200°C/400°F; regulate with the vents and lid during the baking time, if needed). Cook for 50 minutes or until the filling has just set – it will continue to cook in the residual heat after it has been removed from the barbecue.

Leave the tart to rest for at least 2 hours before transferring to a large plate and slicing to serve.

Serves about 6

You'll also need a 24cm (9½in) loose-based tart (flan) tin, two lumps of hardwood and a length of soaked wooden plank

plain (all-purpose) flour, for dusting

1 quantity Sweet pastry (see page 247), at room temperature

300g (10½oz) good-quality milk chocolate buttons

200g (¾ cup) unsalted butter, melted, plus extra for greasing the tin

5 free-range eggs

50g (¼ cup) caster (superfine) sugar, plus extra for dusting

5 apricots, cut in half and stones removed

Grilled and barbecued autumn fruit with honey sabayon and thyme

Autumn-time sees an abundance of delicious fruit to enjoy, such as apples, pears and quince. Because these are slightly more robust, they work particularly well grilled on the barbecue. The thyme may seem an unusual edition in a dessert recipe, but its fragrance goes brilliantly with the fruit and sweet honey sabayon.

Light the barbecue and set for direct cooking.

Wrap the quince in foil. When the coals are ashen-grey, use long-handled tongs to carefully nestle the parcel into them, making sure it's fully covered with the coals and ash. Close the lid and leave for 40 minutes or until cooked.

Quarter the apple and pear, core them and squeeze a few drops of lemon juice over them, rubbing it over the cut surfaces to prevent them from turning brown. Spread out the apple, pear and plums on a large plate and place in the fridge for 20 minutes to dry them slightly.

Pour half the honey and 5 sprigs of the thyme into a small saucepan, along with 2 tablespoons water. Bring to the boil over low–medium heat on the stovetop and simmer for 5 minutes to infuse, then set aside. Pick the leaves from the rest of the thyme, reserving the stalks for the barbecue.

For the sabayon, whisk together the egg yolks, Marsala, thyme leaves and the remaining honey in a large heatproof bowl. Set the bowl over a pan of simmering water and whisk constantly (hand-held electric beaters are good for this) until the mixture thickens and increases in volume; it's important to keep whisking, so the mixture doesn't 'cook' on the base of the bowl, scrambling the egg yolks. When it's ready, the sabayon should be light, pale and airy. Reserve and keep warm.

Brush the apple, pear and plums with the thyme syrup. Throw the reserved thyme stalks onto the charcoal to smoke, place the fruit on the grill and close the lid of the barbecue. Cook for 5 minutes or until lightly charred, then turn over and brush with more thyme syrup. Cook the plums for a further 3 minutes, and the apple and pear for about 5 minutes, or until they are all soft and charred.

Meanwhile, check that the quince is cooked through and tender – a knife should glide in without any resistance – then leave to cool for 5 minutes before removing the foil. Cut the quince into quarters and remove the core with a small knife or spoon, then drizzle the quince quarters with thyme syrup.

If the skin of the fruit looks overly charred, just peel it off. Serve with the sabayon and any remaining thyme syrup.

Serves 4

1 medium quince
1 large apple, such as Braeburn, Cox's Orange Pippin or Ruben
1 large pear, such as Packham, Comice or Anjou
½ lemon
2 plums, such as Victoria, halved and stoned
150ml (⅔ cup) runny honey
½ small bunch thyme
4 free-range egg yolks
50ml (2½ Tbsp) Marsala or sweet white wine

BASICS

BASICS

Brines and cures

Salting and brining are age-old processes that were used to preserve meat and fish in the days before refrigeration, as salt naturally stops bacteria from growing by dehydrating the cells in the proteins. We now mainly use this process to add intrinsic seasoning and flavour to whatever we are working with. Due to salt's dehydrating properties, it also changes the texture of proteins and makes them easier to cook when grilling or pan-roasting.

Salting is an important part of the cold-smoking process, particularly if what you are cold-smoking won't be cooked afterwards.

We usually dilute wet brines before using them for larger cuts, such as a whole chicken, so the meat can spend longer in the brine without becoming too salty. The recipes include diluting instructions where needed.

Make sure any containers you use for brining are non-reactive – that is, not aluminium – as this can react with the brine and taint the meat.

Dry fish cure

Makes about 500g (1lb 2oz)
250g (1¼ cups) coarse sea salt
250g (1¼ cups) caster (superfine) sugar
finely grated zest ½ lemon
½ tsp fennel seeds, crushed
¼ tsp black peppercorns, crushed

Mix everything together, then use to cure fish as per the recipe requirements. This can be stored in an airtight container for 3 months.

Blackening rub

Makes about 100g (3½oz)

80g (3oz) smoked hot paprika
2 cloves garlic, finely grated
1 tsp thyme leaves, finely chopped
1½ Tbsp dark muscovado (brown) sugar
2½ tsp coarse sea salt

Mix everything together in a bowl. This will keep in an airtight container for 3 months.

Brine for red meat – duck, lamb, beef, game

Makes about 1L (4¼ cups)

100g (½ cup) coarse sea salt
50g (¼ cup) demerara (brown) sugar
1 Tbsp honey
2 bay leaves
8 black peppercorns
4 cloves

Place all the ingredients in a medium non-reactive saucepan with 1 litre (4¼ cups) of water. Slowly bring to the boil, stirring as you go to dissolve the salt and sugar. Remove from the heat and allow to cool before using.

Brine for white meat – chicken and pork

Makes about 1L (4¼ cups)

100g (½ cup) coarse sea salt
50g (¼ cup) caster (superfine) sugar
zest of 1 lemon, peeled off in long strips
2 bay leaves
1 tsp coriander seeds
1 tsp fennel seeds

Place all the ingredients in a medium non-reactive saucepan with 1 litre (4¼ cups) of water. Slowly bring to the boil, stirring as you go to dissolve the salt and sugar. Remove from the heat and allow to cool before using.

Smoked salt

Smoked salt is a fantastic condiment to have on hand for when you want to add a little smoky nuance and a crunch. I love it on grilled steaks.

Makes about 250g (9oz)

You'll also need 2 lumps of hardwood and a length of soaked wooden plank

250g (9oz) Maldon salt or other flaky sea salt

Light the barbecue and set for direct/indirect cooking. Place the lumps of wood onto the ashen coals to start smoking, and set the plank on the grill in the indirect heat zone.

Spread the salt evenly over a baking sheet, then place on the plank and close the lid of the barbecue. Hot-smoke the salt for 1 hour or until it has turned a dark brown colour.

Remove from the barbecue and leave to cool before transferring the salt to a sealed container. The flavour of the smoked salt will improve and balance after 24 hours of resting time. This keeps very well!

Smoked butter

As this will keep well in the fridge for several weeks, even improving in flavour, I recommend you smoke two packs of butter at a time. You'll be surprised how quickly it gets used up!

Makes 500g (about 1lb)

You'll also need a cold-smoking device and some wood chips

500g (about 1lb) cold unsalted butter

Set up the cold-smoking device in the barbecue with the wood chips and get it going.

Dice the butter evenly and lay it out on a baking sheet in a single layer. Place the sheet on the rack in the barbecue, close the lid and vent and cold-smoke the butter for 1 hour. Transfer the butter to a container, cover and leave in the fridge for at least 2 hours before using.

Chorizo ketchup

Here is my spicy version of the classic tomato ketchup. The chorizo adds an interesting, smoky tang. This is great with burgers, breakfasts, grilled fish and just about everything else!

<u>Makes about ½L (4¼ cups)</u>
½ large red (bell) pepper, cored, deseeded and sliced
½ red onion, chopped
2 garlic cloves, chopped
1 red chilli, finely chopped
150g (5½ oz) spicy cooking chorizo, peeled and finely diced
½ Tbsp ground cumin
1 Tbsp smoked hot paprika
750g (1lb 10oz) ripe plum tomatoes, cut into quarters
1 Tbsp tomato purée (paste)
50ml (3½ Tbsp) cider vinegar or white wine vinegar
50g (¼ cup) demerara (brown) sugar
olive oil, for cooking
sea salt and black pepper

Light the barbecue and set for direct/indirect cooking.

Place a saucepan on the barbecue in the direct heat zone and add a lug of olive oil. Add the pepper, onion, garlic and chilli and cook, stirring, for 7–8 minutes until softened. Now add the chorizo, cumin and paprika and cook, stirring, for 10 minute, or until the chorizo and spices are cooked and the natural fat from the chorizo has been released.

Stir in the tomatoes, tomato purée, vinegar and sugar, then move the pan to the indirect heat zone and cook for about 1–1½ hours, stirring every so often, until the ketchup is rich and thick. Season to taste with salt and pepper.

The ketchup will keep for approximately 2 weeks in a sealed container or jar in the fridge.

Alioli

Alioli is simply a mayonnaise flavoured with garlic. This simple sauce is incredibly versatile and a great base for adding your favourite flavours – chopped fresh herbs, grain mustard, chilli, horseradish, you name it.

Makes 200ml (about ¾ cup)
1 large free-range egg yolk
½ garlic clove, very finely chopped
1 small teaspoon Dijon mustard
100ml (generous ⅓ cup) vegetable oil
100ml (generous ⅓ cup) extra virgin olive oil
white wine vinegar, to taste
lemon juice, to taste
sea salt and white pepper

In a bowl, whisk the egg yolk with the garlic and mustard. Slowly add the oils, whisking constantly to emulsify. When all the oil has been added, season with salt and pepper and add vinegar and lemon juice to taste.

Mojo verde

This exotic salsa hails from the Canary Islands where the North-African influence on food and culture is prominent. I use this on most things but it's especially recommended on grilled meats – straight from the BBQ, the hot flesh of the meat absorbing the hot, piquant flavours of the salsa on contact.

Makes about 400ml (1¾ cups)
1 small bunch flat-leaf parsley
1 small bunch coriander (cilantro)
½ bunch mint
1 garlic clove, peeled
1 tsp ground cumin
1 green chilli, deseeded
50ml (3½ Tbsp) red wine vinegar
120ml (½ cup) extra virgin olive oil
sea salt and black pepper, for seasoning

Place all the ingredients except the oil and seasoning into a food processor and start to process. Gradually pour in the oil until you have a thick green purée. Season to taste.

Crunchy shallot and garlic salsa cruda

This really simple salsa is an ace accompaniment to grilled meats and fish, adding texture, freshness and a punch of flavour.

Makes 50–60g (about 4 Tbsp)

1 large banana shallot, or 2 medium-sized ones, finely chopped
1 red chilli, deseeded and finely chopped
2 garlic cloves, finely chopped
2 Tbsp finely chopped flat-leaf parsley
2 Tbsp olive oil
juice of ½ lemon
sea salt and black pepper

Just mix all the ingredients together, seasoning to taste and adding the lemon juice at the last minute.

Sweet pastry

My pastry stalwart, this recipe has been with me for many years. It's a classic and makes the best, crispest pastry for tarts.

Makes enough for one 20cm (8in) tart

250g (1¾ cups) plain (all-purpose) flour, plus extra for dusting
50g (⅓ cup) icing (confectioners') sugar
pinch of salt
125g (½ cup) unsalted butter, cut into cubes
1 egg, lightly beaten
4 tsp full-cream (whole) milk

Sift the flour, sugar and salt into a bowl, then add the butter and rub in to form rough crumbs. Add the egg and milk and mix to incorporate. Bring the dough together into a ball and dust lightly with flour, then wrap in cling film and chill for at least 30 minutes. Bring the pastry back to room temperature before rolling it out.

Smoked bitter chocolate

Smoked chocolate is a revelation, whether you eat it raw or melted and cooked into a pudding. At Ember Yard, we tried several methods and types of chocolate but found that those with a cocoa content of 70% or more works best. I've used pistols (buttons) as they are all the same size, so they absorb the smoke evenly. It's imperative that you leave the chocolate for 24 hours after smoking to allow the flavours to settle and balance.

Makes about 250g (9oz)

You'll also need a cold-smoking device and some oak wood dust
250g (9oz) bitter chocolate (at least 70% cocoa) buttons, or a block cut
  into small, even-sized chunks

Set up the cold-smoking device in the barbecue with the wood dust and get it going.

Place the chocolate in a single layer on a baking sheet. Transfer to the barbecue, then close the lid and vent and cold-smoke the chocolate for 45 minutes. Transfer the chocolate to a container, seal and leave for 24 hours before using.

Salted caramel

Salted caramel has become a food fashion icon of late and is ubiquitous on menus up and down the land. I have to say I absolutely love the combination (call me a fashion victim if you like) of sweet, burnt caramel and salt. It's one of those very few flavours that send your taste buds to heaven and back.

Makes about 350ml (1½ cups)

250g (1⅓ cups) golden caster (superfine) sugar
120ml (½ cup) double (heavy) cream
25g (1½ Tbsp) unsalted butter
½ tsp sea salt flakes

Place the sugar and 80ml (⅓ cup) water in a small heavy-based saucepan. Bring to the boil over medium heat and cook until you have a deep golden-brown syrup. Don't stir it, or the sugar might re-crystallize, but swirl the pan every so often.

Remove the pan from the heat and pour in the cream (be careful – it will spit). Stir to incorporate, then whisk in the butter and salt. This will keep for up to 2 weeks in the fridge.

SUPPLIERS OF WOOD, CHARCOAL AND BARBECUES

UK

When sourcing charcoal, a good starting point is the fairly ubiquitous Big K Products, which is leaning more and more towards environmentally friendly products. As well as offering quality charcoal, including a new variety of sustainable lump-wood charcoal, they supply compressed cardboard/wax firelighters that are super eco-friendly. However, because their charcoal comes from woodlands across South America and Africa, it needs to be heavier so it doesn't break up in transit; this is achieved by distilling it of impurities to a lesser degree. The downside is that when you burn this charcoal on your grill, the remaining gases are released, which can adversely affect the charcoal flavour on your food.

English woodland-produced charcoal is becoming more and more popular; some supermarkets have even started to stock it now. And by ordering from specialist suppliers online, it's very easy to get deliveries up and down the country.

bigk.co.uk
Charcoal, lighters, lump wood

londonlogco.com
English charcoal, single species, lump wood – and advice

hotsmoked.co.uk
Large selection of smoking chips, ceramic grills, smokers and accessories

amazon.co.uk
Charcoal, lump wood, smoking chips, barbecues/grills, accessories

treewoodcharcoal.com
British charcoal, lump wood and smoking chips

weberbbq.co.uk
Barbecues/grills, smokers and accessories

drumbecue.co.uk
Barbecues/grills, smokers, chimney starters

biggreenegg.co.uk
Barbecues/grills, charcoal, smoking chips

US and Canada

atbbq.com
Barbecues/grills, charcoal, smoking chips, chimney starters

mapleleafcharcoal.com
Canadian maple and other lump wood, charcoal

rockwoodcharcoal.com
Charcoal from Missouri

realmontanacharcoal.net
Smoking wood and charcoal

weber.com
Barbecues/grills, smokers and accessories

biggreenegg.com
Barbecues/grills, charcoal, smoking chips

amazon.com
Charcoal, lump wood, smoking chips, barbecues/grills, accessories

INDEX

ACKNOWLEDGMENTS

This book couldn't have happened without the unfailing energy and enthusiasm of Jacques Fourie, my head chef at Ember Yard and an inspiration for this book. Jacques was also intrinsic in some of the beautiful recipes in this book. Always ready with a cup of green tea for me at 7.30am – a priority on recipe testing days – and managing to keep them coming, endlessly, whilst juggling one hundred recipes.

To my lovely wife Nykeeta, who puts up with all my foodie nonsense and is my biggest (constructive) critic and the best friend and partner a husband could want. Also chief recipe tester in our house, along with Piglet. I love you both dearly.

Thanks to Simon Mullins, co-founder of Salt Yard Group. Thanks for the wine knowledge in these pages, the brilliant support and for allowing me to get on with this book. I thoroughly enjoy our working dynamic and look forward to more restaurant adventures alongside you.

Mark Parr (Lord Logs) of London Log Company (londonlogco.com) who has supported this project (and Ember Yard) from Day One, not just with his amazing charcoal and wood, but with his vision, locations and endless enthusiasm. He's a great person to know in the world of charcoal and a lovely guy to boot.

To the amazing team that helped get this project to the finishing line: Martine Carter at Sauce Management; Céline Hughes, Helen Lewis and Nikki Ellis and the team at Quadrille; Kris Kirkham for his brilliant photography and his love of a glass of rosé; Tamzin Ferdinando for her wonderful props; all my suppliers who supply the best produce in the UK, especially George at Rare Breed Meat Company, Brindisa, Deli Station, Direct Seafoods and Debono Foods.

Our PR team at Sauce: Jo, Nicky, Laura and Fran who have been intrinsic in our PR strategy.

All my teams at the restaurant who have in some way or another helped in the process of this book and are always an inspiration. They say that you are only as good as your team and these words are very true indeed. Everything we do is a team effort.

My mentors and great friends Jason Atherton, Stephen Terry and Mark Sargeant – fantastic chefs and even nicer people. I undoubtedly would not be where I am today or have written this book without your inspiration and influence. How you didn't kill me in the process I don't know.

All our foodie friends and journalists who have helped us over the years and written such nice words.

Finally, all our restaurant's customers who have been coming for years and continue to come back. We have such a loyal following and we so appreciate it.

Publishing Director: Sarah Lavelle
Creative Director: Helen Lewis
Senior Editor: Céline Hughes
Designer: Nicola Ellis
Photographer: Kris Kirkham
Prop Stylist: Tamzin Ferdinando
Illustrator: Martin Hargreaves
Production: Vincent Smith, Stephen Lang

First published in 2016 by
Quadrille Publishing
Pentagon House
52–54 Southwark Street
London SE1 1UN
www.quadrille.co.uk

Quadrille is an imprint of Hardie Grant
www.hardiegrant.com.au

Reprinted in 2016 (four times)
10 9 8 7 6 5

Text © 2016 Ben Tish
All photography © 2016 Kris Kirkham
Illustration © 2016 Martin Hargreaves
Design and layout © 2016 Quadrille Publishing

Cataloguing in Publication Data: a catalogue record for this book is available from the British Library.

ISBN: 978 184949 715 2

Printed in China